THE
HAIRBRUSH
AND THE
SHOE

THE
HAIRBRUSH
AND THE
SHOE

A TRUE
GHOST STORY

JEANNE D. STANTON

SparkPress, a BookSparks imprint
A Division of SparkPoint Studio, LLC

Published by SparkPress, a BookSparks imprint,
A division of SparkPoint Studio, LLC
Phoenix, Arizona, USA, 85007
www.gosparkpress.com

Published 2020

Printed in the United States of America

ISBN: 978-1-68463-034-9 (pbk)
ISBN: 978-1-68463-035-6 (e-bk)
Library of Congress Control Number: 2019913850

Formatting by Katherine Lloyd, The DESK

For My Grandmother,

Evangeline O'Daniel Deschamps

CONTENTS

❧

CHAPTER ONE

A SENSIBLE WOMAN

"There's no such thing as ghosts!" a male friend sputtered when I mentioned that we had a ghost in our house. "Surely you don't believe in such nonsense!"

"Why not?" I should have answered, since I'd experienced thirty years' worth of having things moved around, the piano played at odd hours, and people pushed on the stairs, all by an unseen hand. But instead I just mumbled something and changed the subject, because I felt embarrassed and unwilling to assert my point of view. Ghosts and belief in them are generally regarded as the realm of charlatans and crackpots. While I could have cited William James, Charles Dickens, and Arthur Conan Doyle as being among those who believed in "such nonsense," he might have countered that their perceptions were formed at a time when most people still believed in God and afterlife, and that they would feel differently today.

Before we moved into our 1875 house, I hadn't thought much about ghosts, but if asked, I would have said that ghosts are a possibility. As a child growing up Catholic, I was told that I had a guardian angel, and although I no longer practice Catholicism,

I have somehow been unable to relinquish belief in that angel. In my mind angels and ghosts are of a piece, both being invisible and part of the great unknown. Thus my position with respect to ghosts has always been, why not?

I am not talking about the lunatic fringe—ghouls, vampires, zombies, or the kinds of demonic creatures conjured up by authors like Stephen King. For me a ghost is simply the spirit of some ordinary person who has died. My notion of what a ghost is was formed in the same way I suspect most people's has been, by writers of stories with ghosts in them—starting with Dickens's *Christmas Carol* and proceeding to plays by William Shakespeare—where spirits of dead people like Marley and Banquo, having a bone to pick, return after death to frighten the wits out of whoever had annoyed or wronged them while they were living.

There is, of course, a large subculture of people who *do* believe in ghosts: mediums, psychics, members of the clergy who do exorcisms. I can't endorse any of these groups or vouch for their abilities, being unable to see or communicate with spirits myself. While I have friends who have consulted psychics and swear by their predictive powers, I know there are many examples of frauds and con artists who fake their ability to read minds and communicate with the dead. I only say that I believe in the possibility of ghosts, and I say this because of what has happened in our house. And while my family snickered at my ghost stories at first, eventually they all came around, as they, too, experienced the inexplicable.

My story begins with a hairbrush and ends with a shoe. The brush disappeared from a fireplace mantel one winter morning and then turned up midsummer in a place no one I knew had put it. The shoe was gone for little more than an hour, last seen under a crib and, after a determined search, found in a place where, once again, no one I knew had put it. Neither the brush nor the shoe had moved very far, only from one part of a room to another. What was odd was that they moved at all, since no member of our household was involved in, or even observed, their transfer.

Who, or what, moved the hairbrush? That was the question I asked upon finding it, and continued to ask for the next thirty years. And why, I also began to wonder, did things I had lost—ordinary stuff like keys, glasses, pieces of mail—usually turn up in a place I might have put them but felt sure I hadn't? A lost house key, for example, might turn up months later in a coat pocket, but it was a coat I couldn't remember wearing.

Unable to find any rational explanation for how the hair-brush had disappeared while I was still in the room, and further mystified by the lost-but-then-found phenomena, as well as the occasional sound effects (a door slamming, footsteps on the stairs), I decided, for lack of a better idea, that we must have a ghost. Old houses are supposed to have ghosts! My daughters snickered, and my husband rolled his eyes whenever I voiced this explanation.

There were long periods when nothing happened, and my blaming the ghost whenever I couldn't find something began to seem silly even to me. Then, years later, long after the hairbrush disappeared, an incident occurred that was entirely different in character: a worker in the house was pushed by something invisible. This unnerved me. My crediting a ghost with household mischief had been a default position, but now my blasé attitude shifted to alarmed curiosity. Did we *really* have a ghost living with us?

Determined to get to the bottom of the ghost business, I felt I first needed to learn what I could about what ghosts really are and how they are supposed to behave. As a former author of case studies at Harvard Business School, where I chronicled managerial problems, I have remained a writer of nonfiction whose raw material is mostly facts (including facts that may be obscure, unknown, discredited, or forgotten). While I'm interested in context and opinion, ultimately my concern is to test assumptions and perceptions and to get at the truth of things. My starting questions, then, were straightforward: What is a ghost? Is it possible they exist? If so, do we have one? Later I would expand my inquiry to ask, who might our ghost be (or formerly have been)?

The internet and several books I found in the library answered the first questions pretty quickly, confirming my impression that ghosts are supposed to be the spirits of real people, now dead, who remain near the site of their death. Their behavior as ghosts is consistent with their behavior and character while alive. Typically ghosts have unfinished business, usually involving justice or revenge, or they have died suddenly and are unprepared to leave for what is generally referred to as "the other side."

This all seemed consistent with what I had learned from my more literary reading, as well as from popular treatments like the movie *Ghosts*. What struck me as new, though, as I read more widely among psychics, spiritualists, and the like, was a shared belief that all of us, when we die, have a choice: to move on, or not to move on. For authors and practitioners in the ghost field, not moving on was an aberration, an ultimately futile gesture, since it prolonged whatever misery or discomfort life had provided, and the job of any self-respecting medium or ghost buster was to convince the ghosts they contacted to get over it and move to the other side.

Answering my question about the possibility of our own ghost would, according to what I read, likely require investigation by a professional, a medium or psychic capable of seeing and communicating with spirits. My library sources on ghost proto-col explained that these were people with a rare set of abilities generally referred to as a sixth sense. This, too, was consistent with my existing impressions, as the term is commonly used to describe people with uncanny perception. What the sixth sense really means, I learned, is that certain people are clairvoyant–another familiar term in general use–possessing a rare set of abilities that allow them not only to see but to establish contact with spirits and to communicate telepathically.

As I read further, and eventually began sampling the pleth-ora of ghost-hunting programs on TV, I realized I had entered a new world, a great, shaggy area referred to as the "paranormal." It was like falling down Alice's rabbit hole, and everything was outsize, misshapen, and generally surreal. This particular rab-bit hole housed an astonishingly large and diverse subculture, with its own history, practitioners, and modes of communication (séances, planchettes, extra sensory perception). The paranormal constituency, I discovered, is a cross section of global humanity, with all classes, professions, and religions represented. In the United States and England, this population has included philoso-phers, scientists, theologians, writers, and artists (William James is a prominent example of the educated, intellectual class) as well as many members of the working classes (one of the first and most successful of the reality television programs, *Ghost Hunters*, is based on the paranormal work of two plumbers from Rhode Island, Jason Hawes and Grant Wilson).

While I was delighted to find myself in the company of William James, I wasn't so willing to embrace the paranormal professionals–clairvoyants, mediums, psychics–who play an active role in providing whatever communication we have with ghosts. Much of the literature I found on mediums and their practice dealt with frauds, such as the fakes operating after the

Civil War, who rounded up grieving widows for séances and brought them news from dead relatives via clever manipulation of sound and light. Not having the requisite sixth sense myself, there was no way I could assess their credibility. I felt more comfortable with a second tier of professionals represented by the television ghost busters, who do not claim to have a sixth sense and instead use mechanical devices to detect the presence of spirits.

When I was writing cases, if a management problem existed in a company whose business was very esoteric or complex, I often wrote an industry note, a separate document describing the general nature of the business—how it had evolved, what raw materials or processes it required, who were its clients and competitors, typical expense categories, and so on. Viewing the paranormal in this way, I found the area to be extremely esoteric for those of us not actively involved. I had read about basic concepts and tenets of the spirit world and learned a new vocabulary, words like *poltergeist* and *revenant*. There were professionals and amateurs, techniques and special equipment. The paranormal world even has its own R&D function, in the form of scientific experiments that continue at the Society for Psychical Research in London, and in a less rigorous form via the anecdotal data furnished by hundreds of ghost-hunting groups and clubs. In fact, while I expected to find a preponderance of lore and superstition during my research into the topic of ghosts, I was amazed to discover a consistent thread of scientific inquiry.

Digging around the library and the web was providing me with all the information I needed about spirits and their behavior, but I wasn't getting any closer to my own ghost. If ghosts existed, and we had one, who was it? Who had it been in life, and why was it hanging around?

From earlier research into our house's ownership, I knew,

or thought I knew, who had lived in it before us. The original owner, Dr. Putnam, was a prominent pediatrician who lived here with his wife and three children for thirty-five years. The elderly doctor had died at home after a brief illness; his widow moved a block away to a smaller house and died twelve years later. They were followed by a young couple with three daughters who left for the suburbs after ten years. We bought the house from another doctor, whose family had occupied it for fifty years; this doctor and his wife, both elderly and infirm, died several years after moving out. I knew of no circumstances that would have prompted them to linger in this world after death, as they died at an advanced age of natural causes.

The families prior to us had kept servants, among them young women from Ireland and rural areas of New England. When we first looked at our house, the wife, while showing us around, had referred to the cook, housekeeper, and maids who used to occupy small rooms on the top floor. I definitely preferred that our ghost be a young, anonymous housemaid, someone I could picture only vaguely, had never met, and couldn't ever know much about.

Long-term residents included the original owner's brother and his family, a spinster sister, her widowed friend, the friend's young son, and various adult children. All were potential candidates for resident ghost. Should I do the research, track each one back to their date of death, and try to deduce the circumstances? Or should I take the less labor-intensive route and engage a psychic?

Years ago I toured the Ford Motor Company's historic Rouge plant in Dearborn, Michigan. It was an extraordinary experience, following a huge ingot of molten iron ore from the furnace to the end of the production process, where the ore, forged into steel, emerged as a finished car that was driven off the end of the assembly line. If I had been writing an industry note on the auto industry, I could have described the smelting process, listed the six hundred separate operations required to transform a lump of steel into a car, and described the innovative production system that coordinated workers and conveyor belt so that each part was where it needed to be at exactly the right moment.

The world of the paranormal was nothing like this or any other industry, having no visible product or process, no regularity or predictable outcome. Despite the prodigious number of believers, for most of the population paranormal "evidence" is all hearsay—random, ephemeral, mysterious at best to those not equipped with a sixth sense. As an explorer in this vast new world, I would have to suspend disbelief, take everything in, and then try to sort it all out.

CHAPTER TWO

❧

A BRIEF HISTORY OF INEXPLICABLE EVENTS

It was early on a winter Monday morning when the hairbrush disappeared. Five-year-old Laura had just come downstairs, and I was rushing to get her ready for school. I picked up the hairbrush from where I kept it on the bedroom mantel and was about to start working through the tangles in her long hair, a morning ritual we both hated, when the phone rang.

Laura darted out the bedroom door as soon as I turned and crossed the room to answer the phone. The caller was a car-pool colleague with a question about the week's schedule. Hanging up, I called to Laura as I hurried to retrieve the hairbrush. It wasn't on the mantel. I knew I had left it there, but I began looking around the room anyway, on the night table, on the dresser, in the bed, even under the bed. I went over the same territory several times.

At the end of the week, the hairbrush was still missing, so I bought a new one. What had happened to the old brush, which seemed to have vaporized while I was talking on the phone, was a mystery. I had looked; our cleaning lady, Rita, had been asked to look; and my husband, Don, had shuffled through the books and papers on his side of the bed. There was no sign of it.

Months later, wanting to check the expiration date on my passport, I opened the lid of an antique secretary desk that sits between the two bedroom windows. There, stuffed in a cubbyhole, was the missing hairbrush. For a moment I was unable to grasp what I saw, and I just stood and stared, my perceptual facilities jammed. This mental static was followed by a prickly chill as I began to absorb the fact of the brush being in a place where it was impossible for it to be. How did it get inside the desk? Someone had to have put it there, but who?

I kept the discovery of the missing brush to myself. I was too puzzled, too disconcerted, and I didn't want to hear from my husband that it was just my absentmindedness, that I'd opened the desk for some reason and left it there. This two-hundred-year-old desk, painted red and decorated in the chinoiserie style with tiny kimono-clad women and dwarf pines, was very fragile and rarely opened. We kept important papers inside—birth certificates, the deed to the house, passports. No, I had not opened the lid and absentmindedly shoved the hairbrush way back in a cubbyhole among old letters and documents. And Laura had run out of the room the minute the phone rang. It had been placed there—hidden there—by a purposeful hand.

As soon as we moved into the five-story house, I had begun to lose things, the Victorian building being full of nooks and crannies, and I being inclined to stash or drop whatever was in my hands when the phone or doorbell rang. Now I began to pay much closer attention when objects went missing. If something wasn't where I was sure I had left it, I did a quick search, and if I didn't find it right away, I waited. Eventually the lost item would reappear. An earring might be in a corner of the top drawer where I had already looked, but perhaps not carefully enough.

My glasses would reappear tucked into a magazine, a place I might well have left them but knew I hadn't.

Then a day came when I was late for work and couldn't find my keys. Don, noting my exasperated flapping about, asked what was wrong. "I left my keys right here," I blurted, slapping my palm down on the hall table, "but the ghost took them!" Don looked at me like I had mutated into someone he didn't know. The silence that followed my outburst continued for several seconds while he stared, then inched around me and retreated down the stairs and out the front door. I fetched my extra set of keys and proceeded on my own way. But the cat was out of the bag, and from then on if I couldn't find something, I just said, matter-of-factly, "The ghost took it."

My willingness to accept otherworldly phenomena proved anathema to my husband, who could not reconcile the image of his commonsensical wife with the kind of lunatic female who believed in ghosts. Laura and her little sister, Elizabeth, however, loved the idea and began crediting the ghost whenever any of us, but usually me, couldn't find something. "Oh, Mom can't find her checkbook. The ghost must have taken it," Laura would say, giggling. "Where are my new gym socks? Does the ghost have them?" I didn't mind. That there was a ghost seemed reasonable to me. Why not? Old houses like ours are supposed to have ghosts.

Meanwhile, objects continued to be moved, and noises were made that could be explained, sort of, but not really. One incident, which occurred roughly a year after my discovery of the hairbrush, merited a call to the police and frightened us badly. It was a weeknight, about eleven, and I had just turned off my bedside lamp. As I began to doze off, I heard footsteps coming down the stairs. Laura was a problem sleeper and I expected her to appear in our room momentarily, at which point I would get up, walk her back upstairs, and sit in her room until she settled down. But the footsteps did not stop at our door and I saw a dark shape pass by. "Laura!" I whispered loudly. "Laura! Where are you going?" The steps continued down the stairs and across the hall into the dining room. I jumped out of bed and, leaning over the banister, called, "Laura! Laura!"

"What, Mom? What do you want?" Laura's voice answered me from above, and I looked up to see her in her nightgown, standing outside her bedroom door.

"Nothing, sweetie, I thought I heard you. Go back to bed!" I called up to her. Don was snoring away, and I poked at him furiously. "There's someone in the house!" He jerked awake and together we went out on the landing, listening for footsteps. Nothing. We crept down the stairs and peeked into the dining room, which was empty. When we turned on the light and saw a sideboard drawer pulled open and several serving pieces set out on the table, Don and I rushed back upstairs and called 911.

We were too frightened to go back downstairs, not knowing where the intruder might be lurking, and when the policeman arrived, we threw keys out the window over the front door and he let himself in. Together we began searching the house, all the closets, bathrooms, even going down into the cellar, where Don aimed his flashlight at the narrow space behind the furnace. No one was there. The drawer in the dining room was open but nothing else was disturbed. Where was the burglar? How had he gotten out? And how had he gotten in? The upstairs windows were locked, and those on the lower floors had iron bars.

One window, in the living room, did not have bars, mainly because it was two stories above the street and only a monkey could have gotten up to it. It, too, was closed, but the policeman decided that this was the likely point of entry and exit, which satisfied Don. I had my doubts.

Other incidents were merely puzzling. One evening I was working at the kitchen table when I heard the piano. It wasn't really playing, more like a hand running over the keys in a clumsy glissando. I ran into the living room, which was empty except for the cat, asleep on a chair at the opposite end of the room, exactly as she had been all evening. Don was upstairs and when I called to him, he said that he, too, had heard the piano. "Well," I said, "what do you think of that?" Silence.

One Saturday afternoon, as the girls and I were returning from shopping, Laura saw a woman with dark hair in the laundry room. "What's Rita doing here on Saturday?" she asked, following Elizabeth and me upstairs to the kitchen. I ran back downstairs to the small room that houses the washer and dryer. No one was there. Another time, when we had just returned from a weeklong vacation, Elizabeth asked me why her bed was pulled away from the wall. I went to look. The cast-iron bedstead had been moved out roughly ten inches, the indentations in the carpet where the legs had been still visible. With mattress and box spring, the bed was far too heavy for anyone to move alone. It had to have been the ghost, but was there more than one?

Over the years these kinds of events continued, widely spaced but distinct and inexplicable. Yet everyone continued to treat the ghost's existence as my own private fantasy, with Don refusing to participate in any ghost-related conversation and the girls taking a let's-humor-our-crazy-mother tone. Then a high school teacher of Laura's came to live with us for the summer; we had bought a place in the country where we spent most weekends, and we needed a house sitter.

One evening as I was preparing the girls' dinner, Keith came into the kitchen to thank me for folding his laundry. "What laundry?" I asked. "The laundry I left in the dryer this morning.

Didn't you fold it? Someone did." I hurried downstairs to look. There, on top of the dryer, were neat piles of socks and T-shirts. No one had been home all day.

"It must have been the ghost," Elizabeth said, snickering.

"Oh, do you have a ghost?" Keith seemed genuinely interested.

"I think we do, but no one believes me," I said.

"Why not?" he asked. Keith assured me that ghosts do exist and that no doubt at least one inhabited our 125-year-old house. "Why do you think the dog barks the way he does?" he asked, referring to the fact that our normally placid Scottie would occasionally run into the back hall and bark frantically. "Dogs are very sensitive to ghosts."

This was helpful, but more substantive reinforcement soon came from my daughters, who now began telling their own ghost stories. Laura claimed that while she never saw any ghosts at night, they sometimes made so much noise that they kept her awake. Elizabeth told us how one night, just after she had gotten into bed and turned off her light, something landed on her pillow. Turning her lamp back on, she found a hair band that she had left on a chest across the room.

When Don entered the kitchen, I asked Keith to repeat his story. Leaning against the counter while the rest of us sat around the kitchen table, Don listened to Keith's tale of folded laundry, a tale told not by a fanciful female but by a red-blooded young man who watched *Sunday Night Football.* "Yes," Don said finally, "I think you are right about the ghost, because in the morning it hangs out in our bedroom, over by my dresser."

I was stunned. Not only had Don gone seamlessly from denial to acceptance, but he had also identified the same presence I felt every morning as I sat reading the paper. Occasionally there would be a slight noise, a soft creak, but mostly it was a physical sense I had of something hovering around the area by his side of the bed.

After the laundry folding, nothing happened for some time. Then we began a small construction project that included the installation of a new bar sink. Our neighbor Cheryl, a talented artist who usually works only for decorators, agreed to marbleize the wooden counter. She planned to work over a weekend when we were away; Keith had moved out a month earlier, and the house would be empty.

When I called Cheryl on Monday morning, she was in a tizzy. "I spent all Saturday prepping the surface and then I packed my paints and tools in a canvas tote and left it on the floor. I came back Sunday morning and someone, some idiot, had picked up my bag and set it right where I had painted," she sputtered. "I had to sand the whole thing down and start over. You didn't tell me anyone else was going to be in the house this weekend!"

"Uh . . . no one was," I replied, suspecting that the same ghost who folded laundry might have picked up the bag off the floor. Cheryl and I had discussed ghosts before, as she claimed to have one in her small apartment, a wispy young woman who appeared from time to time near her bathroom door. I broached this possibility.

"Okay, this ghost of yours may have caused the damage," Cheryl said in a new businesslike tone. "I think you need to exorcise what seems to me to be a malevolent spirit. And I know someone who might help."

I was appalled at this suggestion. No! I didn't want to exorcise the ghost. I had never thought of it as destructive, or malevolent, nor did I think of our house as haunted. There simply was this— spirit?—that hung about and moved things from time to time. And while discrete incidents seemed to have decreased—particularly, it occurred to me, since the girls had left for college—I knew it was still around.

After a thirty-year hiatus, I had resumed piano lessons, and each evening before dinner I would go into the living room, sit down at the piano, adjust the lamp, arrange my music, and begin to pick through a Bach prelude. Soon I would feel some other presence. There was always a sound, a slight creaking of wood or a soft snap such as a light bulb sometimes makes, nothing as audible or distinct as a footstep, just barely discernable noises that signaled something moving into and through the room, beginning near the small door to the back hall. I saw nothing. But I had a physical awareness that I can't describe except in the way an artist friend once did as she talked about sculpture. "Painting is on the wall," she had said. "It's two-dimensional. You look at it. But sculpture is three-dimensional, and you interact with it in a different way. You share space with it." That's how it was with the ghost. I knew when it had arrived in the room because I could feel myself sharing space with it.

I didn't want to scare the ghost away. The ghost was like our dog, who had come into our home one Christmas as an unwelcome surprise, a gift from my mother for the girls. I never wanted a dog, but after ten years, I was used to finding him asleep just inside the front door whenever I returned home. On those rare occasions when he wasn't there, the house didn't feel right. It was the same with the ghost, an uninvited but mostly benign presence that somehow kept me company. If it left, I would miss it.

As Cheryl proceeded to tell me about a woman she had worked for who had had an exorcism done at her house, I listened, but I did not write down the name and number she gave me. Perhaps the ghost heard us talking and left anyway, because for the next several years, there was little overt sign of its presence. I'd hear the odd noise—a door banging on the top floor when I knew they all were tightly shut—but the presence I felt while practicing the piano diminished, and I sensed nothing at all in our bedroom.

Then we began a project I had dreamed of for years, the complete gutting and remodeling of what real estate agents call the "master bath," a cramped space off our bedroom with no bathtub, only a shower and a single small sink. The demolition would take almost a week.

Don and I took off for a long weekend in the country once the work began, returning late Monday afternoon. We were surprised to find a pickup truck still parked behind the house, long after the usual three o'clock quitting time. Inside, two of the workmen, Dan and Jeff, were waiting for us.

"I couldn't leave without telling you what happened today," Dan said. Soft-spoken and deferential, with a balding head and thick glasses, Dan is a guy you might not notice except that he is six foot five.

"I was walking up the stairs, just back from lunch," he continued. "About halfway up, maybe eight steps from the landing, something brushed past me, gave me a push on the shoulder, and hissed in my ear, just like this—*sssssssss!*"

"Yeah," Jeff broke in. "I was just behind, and when Dan stopped short, I ran right into him. Then he turned around and his face was white as a sheet!"

Dan repeated his story verbatim, describing how something passed him on the stairs, pushed him, and hissed in his ear. He jabbed his hand in the air to demonstrate the force of the push against his shoulder. The four of us stood quietly for a moment, considering Dan's story.

"Well," I said, "it must have been the ghost. But it's never touched anyone!"

"Yeah, well, I remember you saying once that you've got a ghost here," Dan said. "And I'm fine with that. My aunt has an old colonial house full of ghosts, and they don't bother anyone. But this was amazing. It pushed me really hard!"

"Are you okay?" I asked, wondering if Dan would be back the next day.

"Oh, yeah, fine, just weirded out," he said. "Well, see you tomorrow."

And off they went, leaving Don and me to ponder this dramatic new occurrence. Clearly our renovations had upset the ghost. But who was it? Given the laundry folding and the way it seemed to prefer the back hall and upper floors, I'd always thought of the ghost as a former female servant, probably a girl from Ireland or rural New England who had died during the 1918 influenza epidemic. Now I wondered. Could it be the previous owner, the now-deceased doctor whose family had lived in our house for fifty years? To expand the bathroom, we were ripping apart what had been his dressing room, dismantling the linen cupboard where he kept his shirts, tearing out the metal cabinet that had held his toiletries. Was he angry about the changes we were making? I'd met Dr. Caner, and he was a big man capable of giving Dan a good shove.

Nothing happened after that. The remodeling proceeded as scheduled, and in six weeks we had a new bathroom, spacious and up-to-date. There were no further pushings or hissings, and Dan has continued to do work in our house. He grins broadly when Don asks him to tell us again about the time the ghost pushed him.

For me, however, this episode marked a turning point. Our ghost's prankish behavior had become hostile, and it involved physical contact. While I had no doubt that there was a ghost or some facsimile at large in our house, I'd never given serious thought to what ghosts really are or how they behave. Dan's experience made me want to know much more about who—or what—was living with us.

CHAPTER THREE

MY UNDERCOVER INVESTIGATION

During the next few weeks, I searched the internet and the library for information about ghosts and their behavior. Soon I was so immersed in ghost research that I found myself spending hours reading about aspects of the nether world that had little or nothing to do with my own situation. My research topic was of a breadth I hadn't imagined, going back to the ancient Greeks and encompassing all of the world's cultures and religions, including Christianity. After the Resurrection, for example, there was debate among the disciples about whether it was Jesus himself or his ghost who appeared to them on the road to Emmaus.

A second discovery was how much research I could do alone, when I chose, and in the privacy of my home office. This latter feature proved critical, since once I ventured outside my family, I felt self-conscious about my topic, unwilling to have others know what I was up to. "What are you working on?" was a frequent question among acquaintances who knew I had published a book on career strategies for women and was still actively engaged in writing. "I'm doing research on ghosts" wasn't an answer I was prepared to offer up to people who assumed that my interests pertained to something solid and useful. Fearing I'd be dismissed as having lost it, I embraced secrecy and worked quietly in my home office, huddled over my computer in safe isolation.

Entering the word *ghost* on Google sent me straight to Wikipedia and a daunting quantity of information. I printed sixteen pages of illustrated text and five pages of references that outlined the history and categories of ghosts, lists of spirit-related practices in various countries, and sections on their depiction in art and literature. I read that belief in ghosts and their more illustrious colleagues—angels, deities, demons—was age-old and universal, and that by far the bulk of human effort in this area has been directed toward appeasing spirits believed to have hostile agendas. These efforts ranged from sacrificial rites aimed mostly at deities thought to control some aspect of the future to annual feeding rituals intended to keep dead relatives from getting testy and obstreperous due to hunger. Halloween, which we celebrate today in a revised version—live children go to neighbors' houses demanding candy—nonetheless retains many trappings of its origins; that is, ghost and skeleton costumes intended to evoke the dead and food offered in return for amnesty from "tricks."

The other common theme in ghost history was tragedy and loss, often coupled with revenge, as in the many "white lady" legends that typically feature a romantic tale of rejection and abandonment. Assumed to be bereft, ghosts didn't live in houses; they "haunted" them, lurking about the scene of some tragic and often violent event. And for the living, seeing a ghost was often a portent of death. It all seemed to me very negative and unhappy, far removed from disappearing hairbrushes and mysteriously folded laundry.

Nonetheless, I found the introduction to the language of the ghost milieu enlightening, a way of organizing the random terminology I'd absorbed from movies and novels over the years. A list of synonyms for ghosts included ones I already knew, such as *spirit* and *apparition*, but many others were new to me. *Ghost* is a distinct category in the paranormal lexicon, and the definition of a ghost is very precise: a ghost is the spirit of a formerly living thing. (Whether ghost as a category includes the spirits of animals and trees is not agreed upon.) Also, it seemed important to remember that ghosts, like angels and demons, were mostly invisible, but there the resemblance ended, since angels and demons and deities, despite their taking human form from time to time, never existed as physical entities and therefore cannot be classified as ghosts. Zombies, the things that clump around on shows like *The Walking Dead*, are not ghosts either, being the body without the spirit. Vampires, those perennially popular members of the paranormal world, are a variety of zombie that sucks blood.

There are a number of synonyms for ghost, including *shade*, *spook*, *wraith*, *specter*, *phantom*, *poltergeist*, and *haint*, the latter a term widely used in the southern United States, where ghost stories, or *haint tales*, are a popular storytelling tradition. There are other, more archaic words that I found oddly compelling, either because they prompted personal associations or because they were fun to say. *Revenant* is a term from medieval times for visible zombielike creatures, animated corpses who return to the scene of their death in order to terrorize the living. But when I said the word aloud, "revenant" slid through my lips like a silky whisper, a French word that sounded like "reverie." *Succubus*, which denotes an evil female spirit that preys sexually upon sleeping men, is a harsh, coarse word that when said aloud sounds almost dirty. A *fetch* is the visible ghost or spirit of someone who is alive (though usually not for long). Somehow this word makes me grin.

I was eager to know what ghosts are supposed to look like, since the closest I'd come to seeing what might have been a ghost was the shadow that had passed our bedroom door the night I was awakened by footsteps on the stairs. There seemed to be three major versions of the visible ghost: wispy, transparent shapes that are vaguely human (a concept thought to be based on early interpretations of breath made visible in the cold); cartoonish Casper-the-Friendly-Ghost types, originating in the draped sheeting used for post-Shakespearean ghost costumes, when it seemed desirable to differentiate ghosts visually from the flesh-and-blood characters; and vaporous but fully clothed, recognizable facsimiles of a formerly living person. This latter notion of a ghost's appearance seemed to be most common, no doubt due, it occurred to me, to man's unimaginative tendency to visualize God, angels, the devil, anything we can't see, in his own image.

Because ghosts were mostly thought to be malevolent, and also because Jews and Christians were cautioned that ghosts were likely to be devils in disguise, much of the history of ghosts involves ways of getting rid of them. Allegedly devils (also referred to as demons) are set on obtaining control of a victim's immortal soul. (This bit of information struck a chord, as I had recently visited a museum exhibit in nearby Salem that featured a sound artist who, charged with creating a piece relevant to Salem's nautical history, used an old Scottish ballad that described how a young woman, having lost her lover at sea, was lured to Hades by a devil posing as his ghost.) Devils can be banished by mentioning the name of Jesus Christ, and today as in the distant past, exorcisms and many cleansing rituals include prayer. But even the spirits of ordinary mortals, often close relatives, were feared for their perceived inclination to resent being dead and, unless mollified somehow, to return and wreak havoc upon the living. Keeping dead humans quiet and out of sight involved everything from binding corpses in chains to making offerings of animals or food.

This all seemed very medieval. But I was reminded that, despite Casper and such winsome characters as the ghosts of a fun-loving young couple and their dog who haunted a banker named Topper in the eponymous fifties television comedy, ghosts have continued to be a source of fright, their presence associated with some malignancy, terrifying and horrible, as in Susan Hill's 1983 novel *The Woman in Black*, whose title character is a vengeful ghost who lures young children to their death. A 2005 Gallup Poll found that 32 percent of Americans believe in ghosts, and belief in ghosts and the ability to communicate with the dead increased dramatically in the 1990s. Why? TV shows like *Buffy the Vampire Slayer*? Stephen King? Was it part of the whole Goth thing? I couldn't be sure, but I did know that there was nothing very scary or dramatic about our ghost; if we had one, it was a very basic model, and a retiring one at that.

The ease of generating fascinating facts and figures from the internet had lured me rather far from the subject of my research. I decided to venture out to the library to see if I could find any materials that would help me understand our particular ghost. The venerable Boston Public Library, founded in 1848 and second in size only to the New York Public Library, is several blocks from our house; this is where I go to cure procrastination, since once I am there, materials spread out on a broad oak table, there is little to do except get busy. The new wing, Phillip Johnson's modernist addition to the stately McKim building, has open stacks. Perusing the shelves devoted to philosophy, psychology, and religion, I found, shelved with Sigmund Freud's *Interpretation of Dreams* and Carlos Castaneda's *The Art of Dreaming*, horror stories and tales-from-the-crypt, manuals for ghost hunting, and New Age tracts that explored the nature of afterlife. I finally selected *Relax, It's Only a Ghost*, a slender paperback that appeared to deal with contemporary, housebound ghosts of the sort that might be found in our Boston home, and *Ghosts*, an illustrated history of ghost lore ranging from ancient myth to current popular culture.

The author of *Relax* is a Minnesota-based psychic, a writer and teacher named Echo Bodine, a celebrity among her followers, who has appeared frequently on television and is the author of numerous books. (I later watched an interview on YouTube and found her credible, an attractive blonde matron, articulate and personable in a folksy sort of way.) Bodine claims to possess a rare set of abilities that allow her to see, hear, and communicate with spirits. *Relax*, an early work, reviewed her own career path as a medium, describing how she learned she was psychic and began to accept that she could perceive and communicate with spirits, and how she worked to develop her abilities to a point where she could be helpful to people who were being harassed by ghosts, an occupation commonly referred to as "ghost busting." Called to deal with a variety of situations, where householders are plagued by ghosts ranging from silent, wispy ladies in Victorian dress to muscular demons who physically assault their victims, Bodine asserts that ghosts are merely dead versions of live people, and very much in death as they were in life; most are "unhappy, restless, and harmless." She claims to see ghosts in a room as easily as you and I can see wallpaper, and her job, which she maintains is exhausting, is to convince souls stuck in the usually tragic events of their lives to get over it and move "to the other side."

I was startled to read that Bodine had been introduced to the world of ghosts by a guardian angel and that she was, and continues to be, profoundly Christian, her work an adjunct to her Protestant religious practice. Mediums like Bodine, I learned, are typically mentored by "spirit guides," essentially the paranormal version of guardian angels.

Bodine's book brought me further elucidation with respect to the specialized vocabulary of the spirit world. "Psychics," I learned, are clairvoyant, having a sixth sense that enables them to see and hear more than what is perceptible with the usual five, and are best known for an alleged ability to predict the future. "Mediums" are gifted in the same way, and the main difference between the two, so far as I can tell, is that mediums aspire to a different career path, specializing in communication with the dead. Mediums are the key link between people who are living and people who have died, communicating telepathically; their special language is extrasensory perception, or ESP. Communicating with spirits is a process that requires intense mental and physical effort, as mediums must first allow spirits, who have no physical substance and very low energy, to enter the medium's body and absorb their energy—rather, it seemed to me, like reviving a dead car battery by attaching it to a live one.

The book's title proved misleading, as did the cartoonish child's version of a ghost on the cover, since *Relax, It's Only a Ghost* described twenty of her most grueling jobs and ghosts of the most unsavory sort, including a drinker who had set his house on fire, killing his wife and children; a deranged woman who physically attacked the young women her former boyfriend brought home; and a Vietnam veteran who, refusing to believe he was dead, terrorized the occupants of the house he had owned. Bodine claimed to have confronted and dealt with all of these misfits, even one who tried to push her down a flight of stairs. Her modus operandi is to explore a supposedly haunted house with the lights off, since ghosts, in her experience, give off a light gray energy that she can see more easily in the dark. Once she has located it, Bodine enters into conversation with the ghost, asking about its reasons for remaining behind and then talking through why it would be so much better for the ghost to move on. This can be a lengthy process, with Bodine offering continual advice and encouragement to the earthbound spirit as it moves, oftentimes very haltingly, "into the light." Once it has gone, Bodine finishes up by burning sage leaves, a Native American ritual that she uses to diffuse any remaining negative energy emanating from either the departed ghost or the trembling clients.[1]

I couldn't fathom any of this as relevant to my own situation, couldn't imagine our ghost behaving like any of the horrors Bodine described. Her experiences seemed so bizarre, the ghosts so flagrantly malevolent. If Bodine came to my house, site of harmless mischief, I presumably could take her up to our bedroom, and she would tell me that a young woman with long brown hair, wearing an apron and wielding a feather duster, was hovering about Don's dresser; I would say fine, let's leave now. Let her be. Or she could describe a very tall man with sparse gray hair, dressed in a three-piece tweed suit, arms folded and scowling. That would be the old doctor from whom we bought the house, the bedroom's former occupant, and I would be weirded out, as Dan had put it. I really didn't want to know that our home's former owner was spying on us.

However, Bodine's book combined her personal story with what she titled "Facts about Ghosts," brief segments at the ends of chapters that described an aspect of their nature and behavior. These proved concise and to the point.

The first and most important thing I learned was the very distinct difference between ghosts and spirits. A ghost is the soul of someone who has died but not moved on, while a spirit is the soul of a dead person who has moved on but comes back to visit from time to time. And while spirits tend to return or communicate only when summoned, ghosts are with us whether we want them or not.

The difference between the two, it seemed to me, was the nature of their behavior, given that both are what is left when the physical body has died. The more I thought about it, the more I realized that the two words are mostly used interchangeably. I remembered the reference to Christ's appearance to his disciples and wondered about the exact wording of their conversation. I knew we had several copies of the New Testament at home and thought I knew exactly where to find Laura's confirmation Bible, a fancy edition with a white leather cover, gold lettering, and print so tiny I knew I would also have to find a magnifying glass if I was going to read it. But when I went to the shelf, there was the Oxford Annotated Bible, a 1962 college edition, with my husband's name written on the flyleaf in a feminine hand—clearly a high school graduation gift bestowed by his mother or some other female relative, and I am sure that the pristine volume never made it to college. I found the account of Christ's appearance on the road to Emmaus in Luke 24, describing how he had had to convince his disciples, who "supposed that they saw a spirit," that he was himself, alive, "for a spirit has not flesh and bones as you see that I have." Having not died, Jesus couldn't be a spirit. And he certainly couldn't be a ghost.

Bodine also reported that typically ghosts are tied to the sites of their deaths, are disturbed when their environment is changed, and may seek out one another, in a misery-loves-company sort of way. Poltergeists are ghosts who specialize in moving things.

Given the movement of beds and hairbrushes, we seemed to have a ghost with poltergeist tendencies. While learning this was helpful, I wasn't satisfied, because I still didn't know why our ghost did a lot of other things, like pushing people on the stairs, nor could I explain the long absences or predict how it might behave in the future. And might we have more than one?

My other reference, *Ghosts*, by a British author named Jon Izzard, was a survey of the field, a sort of "Introduction to Ghosts 101," and in cross-checking Bodine's facts with Izzard's, I found the generic information to be in agreement. Izzard, however, did not offer any personal experience, only that of others as provided in the public record, and what he did offer was accompanied by qualifiers such as "people say" and "legend has it."[2] While Izzard clearly was not going to out himself as a believer, I found his book extremely informative, as it covered all the variations of ghosts, described the range of amateurs and professionals who traffic in the paranormal, and offered numerous examples of film and other artistic treatments.

I searched out his definition of poltergeist, a word meaning "noisy ghost" in German. According to Izzard, poltergeists move objects around, make noises, and are usually more mischievous than malicious, and for this reason such ghosts are often thought to be children. Further, many recorded incidents involve teenage girls, and he wrote that some "recurrent spontaneous psychokinesis" may have been going on, *psychokinesis* being the ability of living people to use mental powers to move objects. This was confusing, as I couldn't tell whether he felt that young girls possessed these powers, or that another person was doing the mental moving with a view to terrorizing some hapless adolescent.

Around this time, my husband and I had to make a trip to Delaware to visit his hospitalized father, and at the end of an early evening we returned to our hotel room, and Don turned on the television. A program I'd never seen before, *Ghost Adventures*, was just ending, but the trailer promised a post-investigation interview with the three stars, men who travel around the country investigating allegedly haunted buildings. I grabbed the remote before Don could begin channel surfing for some sports program and sat on the end of the bed, glued to the screen. In order to evoke the atmosphere in which they typically worked—darkness—the three were seated informally, also in a hotel bedroom, with only a flashlight for illumination. The prevailing tone was amateurish and jokey, as the crew and interview subjects bantered with one another and clattered about while they attempted to position themselves in the darkness. But once the interviews began, I was struck by the earnestness of the investigators. With their faces barely lit, each talked about a personal experience with a ghost, a childhood haunting that set them on the ghost-busting path. While no one described exactly what had haunted them, I assumed that their situations were similar to that of the child of a Bodine client, a young girl who claimed she couldn't sleep because of all the people sitting on her bed.

One investigator, a handsome, dark-haired young man with a slow, considered way of speaking, described how he was careful to cleanse himself right after a job, since particularly troublesome ghosts often tried to follow him home. He had a young family to protect and, like Bodine, employed a ritual that involved burning sage leaves. His account was unsettling because it—and he—were so believable.

CHAPTER FOUR

❊

FRAUDS
AND FAMOUS MEN

Believable or not, I reminded myself that a word consistently encountered in my reading about ghosts, spirits, mediums, and the like, was the word *fraud*. Much of what I read seemed consistent, or at least not inconsistent, with what had been going on in our house, and I had to remind myself not to be seduced by writers and practitioners who were part of a long tradition that included charlatans, con artists, and tricksters. A reflexive distrust of the psychic world went back as far as childhood, when my girlfriends and I played at being fortune tellers, dressing up as gypsies with scarves and our mothers' hoop earrings. I recall watching versions of séances on television as a teenager, probably during many late nights spent babysitting. There was always a circular table with a long cloth and a half-dozen or so people sitting around it, holding hands. The person in charge, usually a dark-haired female, would raise her eyes to the ceiling and, while the others kept their eyes shut, intone something like,

"Aunt Maud, Aunt Maud, are you there? Your dear niece Wilma has something she needs to ask you." Soon the table would begin to wobble or tilt, the medium would clamp her eyes shut, and Aunt Maud would make herself known, usually via some rapping noises that served as the spirit world's version of Morse code. This scenario was inevitably revealed to be hokum, as the camera panned to a mustachioed man behind a curtain banging blocks of wood together.

I'd since learned that this stock scenario was based on a format developed during the latter half of the nineteenth century, the heyday of a movement called Spiritualism. Spiritualism was based on a belief that communication with dead people was possible, given a competent medium and a willing spirit. Spiritualism was founded—or perhaps a better word is *invented*—by the Fox sisters of rural upstate New York in 1848, when they claimed to hear rapping in the wall each night after they went to bed. They were able to demonstrate to their family, and then to others, how they could communicate with the spirit who made the sounds—later assumed to be that of a peddler who had been murdered on the property—by asking it questions that could be answered by a varying numbers of raps. Soon they were communicating with other spirits in other locations, satisfying a growing public that there was indeed a community of people who had physically died but who could be accessed by mediums such as the Fox sisters.

The new religion's ready market would soon consist of the thousands of mothers, widows, and assorted family members grieving over sons, husbands, and brothers lost in the Civil War. At its peak Spiritualism had eight million followers in the United States and Britain, all served by mediums, mostly female, who, as the movement grew, embroidered the basic séance format to include various kinds of effects to signal the presence of a conversationally inclined spirit. Apparently many educated, sensible people were taken in by fakers who used light and sound in ways that wouldn't fool a credulous three-year-old today.

While the history and development of Spiritualism wasn't really germane to my research, it did offer a large body of material describing the experience of those who had in the past attempted to communicate with spirits, including how and why the majority failed. (I say *majority* because I found accounts of practitioners who claimed success, seekers of a connection to dead relatives who believed they had found one, despite the lack of serious evidence or documentation.)

Izzard was particularly informative on the subject of Spiritualism. He described how young Kate Fox discovered that she could communicate with the spirit of a dead peddler, who had been murdered and buried beneath her family's home some years earlier. She would clap her hands, and the peddler's spirit (or ghost) would in effect clap back, making corresponding rapping sounds. Kate, together with her sister, Margaret, worked on refining this communication technique, and then began holding séances. They in turn inspired many others, mostly women, to capitalize on their alleged psychic powers. Soon the standard séance format emerged: a table that would levitate, very low lighting, tapping noises, and occasionally floating objects. Sometimes a white, smoky substance would ooze from the medium's ears, nostrils, or mouth. This was called "ectoplasm," and was supposed to be a manifestation of the visiting spirit.

Then, in a twist the Fox girls could not have anticipated, Harry Houdini got involved. I remembered Houdini only as an escape artist, and the picture that came to my mind was of a muscled man, handcuffed and in chains, locked in a trunk, then lowered into deep water. Somehow he got out. But Houdini was both a versatile magician and a staunch defender of the integrity of his profession. He was devoted to exposing frauds and went after mediums with a vengeance. Izzard's book includes a 1925 photograph of Houdini demonstrating how ectoplasm could be faked: Houdini is shown with white smoke or vapor exiting his mouth and congealing in the form of a diaphanous male figure, perched just over his right shoulder.[1]

The photo was taken just before Houdini turned on the lights and revealed the mechanics. His efforts, added to those of several other medium whistle-blowers, discredited Spiritualism sufficiently that membership waned dramatically. But in an even weirder turn of events, the Fox sisters blew the whistle on themselves. After a long career and the creation of a small industry, Margaret Fox confessed that she had faked the original rapping noises, and that at séances she generally produced these sounds by cracking her toe joints. She demonstrated this ability before an audience of two thousand people, all of whom, it is reported, were able to hear the sound she made.

This was an extraordinary story. While I remembered boys in grade school being able to annoy teachers by pulling on their fingers and cracking their knuckles, I'd never heard of cracking toe joints. How was it possible? And if it was, any sound the Fox sisters' toes made would have to be muffled by the layers of Victorian shoe leather, petticoats, and long skirts.

Having suffered from a herniated disk some years ago, I visit a chiropractor every two or three weeks. I decided that on my next visit, I would ask Dr. Ferrara whether or not resonant toe-cracking was possible. When I described the Fox sisters' stratagem, Ferrara, a boyish-looking man of about forty who is also a part-time filmmaker, immediately protested that he had no opinions with respect to whether or not those who professed psychic powers were legitimate. "No," I insisted, "I don't want to know whether or not you believe in what they do. I want to know whether it is possible to crack your own toe joints and make loud noises doing it." To my surprise, Dr. Ferrara waffled. "Well," he responded slowly, "I don't see how people couldn't tell where the sound was coming from."

"Yes," I pressed him, "but could they make the sound?"

"Oh, sure," he said, "people can crack toe joints. And knee joints. Any joints. It's possible."

That would seem to settle it, but I couldn't let go of the Fox sisters, who, despite their late-career confession, inspired the formation of a religion that continues to attract people around the world. Their legacy, at least in terms of numbers, far outshines that of Boston's own Mary Baker Eddy, founder of Christian Science, a religion that now is reported to have less than one hundred thousand members worldwide. Eddy's religious system, which emphasized healing through mental rather than medical processes, had spread rapidly during the same period as Spiritualism, as churches and reading rooms were established around the country. (In my own rural community near Seattle, there was a prim, colonial-style Christian Science church across the street from the elementary school.) Eddy also was a native of rural New England, and she fostered a belief in her ability to heal others through faith in Jesus and focused mental effort, a "laying on of hands." This methodology was partly based on her exposure to mesmeric healing, a practice that incorporated hypnotism. (Both the word and the practice come from Charles Anton Mesmer, an eighteenth-century physician who is said to have effected cures through the use of hypnotism.)

Curious about the Houdini connection—I couldn't understand why he was so determined to go after the Fox sisters, nor did I even know much about who he was—I returned to the library. There were few books on historic figures in the paranormal world, but I did find *Paranormal People*, published by Paul

Chambers in 1998, which included profiles of both Houdini and the Foxes. Houdini, it turned out, had a personal grudge against spiritualists, as he had tried to contact his mother after her death and had decided, during a series of visits to mediums, that their practice was fraudulent. The book also contained a chapter on the Fox sisters which elaborated on their lives and careers, a story that seemed to me not only tragic, but remarkably similar to that of some contemporary celebrities. The young girls were exploited by family members for economic reasons; the prevalence of wine and lack of parental supervision at social gatherings enabled an early introduction to alcohol; and the pressures of being continually on stage led to what we now call substance abuse. The author reports that the two girls were "frequently attacked, both physically and verbally, at their meetings." Constantly challenged by the church and people like Houdini, the sisters finally confessed, Margaret giving a public explanation of their methods. Several years afterward, Kate drank herself to death, and Margaret died alone and destitute less than a year later. Both were buried in pauper's graves.

The part of the Fox sisters' story relevant to my own interests was not their rise and downfall, but the true nature of their abilities: Could Kate and Margaret communicate with the dead, or were they merely skilled at cracking joints? Kate withdrew her confession soon after she made it. The reasons for their late-career acknowledgment of fraud seemed significant. Both were disillusioned and exhausted. Margaret had been married briefly to Elisha Kane, an Arctic explorer who believed that the sisters were perpetrating a fraud and who tried to extract his wife from the family business. Having converted to Catholicism after her marriage, a severely depressed Margaret returned to practice as a medium after her husband's untimely death, leaving the church; thirty years later she returned to Catholicism, stating publicly that her powers were diabolical and the religion of Spiritualism was blasphemous. She did not, I noted, deny that she possessed these "diabolical" powers, and even later claimed that she had confessed due to pressure from the Catholic Church.

This was one part of her story that made perfect sense to me. The Catholic Church not only opposed trafficking with ghosts and spirits for religious reasons, it and other Christian denominations had suffered declining membership. Spiritualism was, in marketing terms, a major competitive threat. And at the time of her confession, Margaret Fox was an embittered alcoholic without friends or family who may or may not have lived a lie.

No one has explained how Houdini worked his magic. Nor has anyone explained how the Fox sisters, particularly Kate, managed other effects, such as floating objects, or for that matter, how the sound from cracking joints could be heard in a hall large enough to hold two thousand people. A prominent British scientist, William Crookes, subjected Kate to every sort of examination short of a strip search, and pronounced her fraud-free. Yet Harry Houdini's wife, who was said to have a pact with her husband that after his death he would communicate from beyond, never heard a word.

I found these stories of people who might have had supernatural powers tantalizing for their potential to prove the existence of spirits, and so terribly frustrating for their failure to do so.

Despite highly publicized evidence of trickery, belief in spirits and the ability of psychics to contact them remained strong, even among highly educated and respected figures. William James, brother of Henry and a celebrated psychologist on the faculty of Harvard, was a believer, although he was thought by his biographers to be susceptible due to his need for comfort after the death of his son. While James ultimately dismissed mediums and their theatrics, he did believe that the dead could make contact with the living, and asked a dear friend who was terminally ill to send him messages after he had died. Unhappily for James, no messages were received.

For my purposes, this all seemed inconclusive, and I wondered where I might find definitive evidence that any one of the many devout spiritualists had made contact with the dead, or even if they had had their personal possessions—that is, hairbrushes and car keys—moved from one corner of a room to another. One evening as I was poking around on the internet looking for more paranormal facts and figures, I came across the Ghost Club, cited as an organization founded in Victorian times to promote scientific examination of otherworldly phenomena. Founders included such prominent scholars and scientists as William James, Arthur Conan Doyle, and Charles Dickens. Hoping that the club's members had generated some useful information, I entered "Ghost Club" and was surprised to be directed to a website. Founded in London in 1862, the Ghost Club still exists. Its members investigate allegedly haunted sites, meet regularly in a private club in London, and publish a quarterly journal. Given an open mind and an interest in the club's research, and completion of a membership application, anyone could join. Well, I certainly had the requisite interest and an open mind, and my husband and I visit London annually. I extracted a credit card from my wallet and signed up for an individual overseas membership (£35, or about $55). I was almost chortling with glee as I filled out the application, never having dreamed that my participation in the paranormal world could be accomplished with such ease of entry. Questions on the application were mostly straightforward: "Have you seen a ghost?" "Do you consider yourself a 'sensitive'?" "Have you any scientific/technical expertise that could prove useful during an investigation?"

Several weeks later, I received a welcome letter and a packet of information including the club objectives—"the investigation and consideration of any subjects not fully understood by science, especially physical and psychical phenomena"—and a caution: "Our investigations are not for entertainment purposes or for thrill seekers." The club's activities included monthly meetings with speakers on paranormal subjects ("Real Ghosts and Hoaxes"); theater outings (*The Woman in Black*); and overnight investigations of reportedly haunted sites (Castle Menzies in Scotland, the Mecca Bingo Hall in Morden). Participants in investigations are advised to wear warm clothing and expect to spend long periods just waiting. It sounded to me a lot like bird watching.

When in London I could visit the club's headquarters; in the meantime I would be kept abreast of paranormal developments and club activities in the organization's quarterly publication, the *Ghost Club Journal*.

It turned out that my new club had a long and illustrious history. Learning of my interest in ghosts, a helpful friend offered me an old program for a production of *The Turn of the Screw*, the dramatization of Henry James's brilliant ghost story. The program notes, written by Joseph Whelan, describe how James based *The Turn of the Screw* on a story told to him by his friend and neighbor Edward Benson, then archbishop of Canterbury. Benson had been one of the group of Trinity College students and faculty joined to study paranormal phenomena. "For reasons personal, philosophical, and intellectual, many at the time were passionately interested in trying to establish communication with the deceased," Whelan writes. What drove this passion was the issue of human mortality, as Charles Darwin had made clear the possibility that when man died, he ceased to exist, period. Without afterlife and, by implication, without God, there was no moral construct, no reason to be moral, no meaning to human life. Members of the Ghost Club sought to refute these implications of Darwinism by finding proof of life after death.

Twenty years later, the original London club, which had been small, private, and secretive, and which had almost faded away after ten years, reinvented itself. Still called the Ghost Club, the group remained small, private, male, and secretive, but met in fancy restaurants to debate the authenticity of alleged supernatural events. Again, the bird-watching analogy struck me, as it seemed as though members were on a quest for something they didn't really expect to find, while fully enjoying the process of looking.

At the same time the Ghost Club was reinvigorated, the Society for Psychical Research was formed to bring scientific research methods to the study of psychical phenomena and events credited to spirits, with the aim of establishing what was fact and what was fancy. This group was open and public with regard to its proceedings and findings. Within ten years the Society had over seven hundred members, including, according to Whelan, "two future Prime Ministers, Nobel Prize–winning scientists, philosophers, and famous writers." Members were charged with "collecting reports of real ghost stories and assessing their veracity." The investigations of alleged paranormal incidents—sightings of apparitions, for example—must have been rigorous, as Whelan reports that of 2,272 cases examined by the Society in 1889, none were found conclusive.

CHAPTER FIVE

ARMCHAIR RESEARCH

Exactly how these early organizations went about disqualifying ghostly events was not clear to me, but surely there were more sophisticated means of ghost investigation available today. A friend had mentioned a television program about ghost busters. I'd never heard of it, but apparently while I'd been watching *Masterpiece Theater*, the rest of the world was watching *Paranormal State*, *Ghost Hunters*, and *Ghost Adventures*, reality-based programs featuring teams of people who investigate haunted sites. I couldn't imagine anything safer than watching people hunt for ghosts on TV, and so I settled in one sunny Friday afternoon with the Travel Channel, which ran episodes of *Ghost Hunters* back-to-back from four until late evening. This was armchair research in the most literal sense.

After viewing one episode of *Ghost Hunters*, during which Rhode Island–based investigators Jason Hawes and Grant Wilson explored a haunted Newport mansion with devices that detect energy fields, I was no wiser. They moved about in the dark, calling out when one or the other sensed something unusual. This went on for what seemed like ages, but by the program's end, nothing visible had appeared. Their investigation of the Reid house, a cheerful-looking yellow building owned by a working-class Rhode Island family, seemed more promising: the four-year-old daughter was terrified in certain rooms; a resident nephew saw shadows in his bedroom; the father claimed to have been attacked while sleeping; and, during a birthday party, two guests who were standing on the porch looked in the dining room window and saw an old gray-haired woman leaning over a birthday cake. Everyone in the family reported shadows and sounds coming from a staircase that opened into a small living room.

Hawes and Wilson went to work, placing cameras and meters that measure electromagnetic fields around the house. As the night wore on, they paced about with flashlights, noting occasional spikes in the meters on the stairs and in various other places. Spoken requests—"Are you standing here with us? Can you tell us your name?"—got no response, although the investigators heard and recorded the faint sound of women laughing.

They also found electrical outlet boxes next to copper tubing. As former plumbers, these two investigators have a professional knowledge of construction, and much of their nighttime work involved examinations of pipes, wires, beams, building materials, and configuration. In their post-investigation meeting with the family, Hawes and Wilson explained that the proximity of copper and electrical elements was creating "an amplified magnetic field" in the affected rooms; shadows on the stairs were coming from the flickering of a nearby television; and the attack in bed was probably an instance of "sleep paralysis," a condition that makes one feel unable to move or breathe just after awakening. The old gray-haired woman was not mentioned.

Next I watched *Ghost Adventures*, starring three personable young men I recognized from the program I had watched in the Delaware hotel room. Zak Bagans, Nick Groff, and Aaron Goodwin travel around the country investigating haunted buildings. Their modus operandi was similar to *Ghost Hunters* and just as dull; they canvassed a former hotel that was the scene of much violence during its heyday as a flophouse, using infrared lighting and detectors. Every so often someone called out, "Whoa! There seems to be something over here!" but aside from needles jumping on their detection devices, there was nothing anyone could see.

After several hours of viewing, I was inclined to dismiss these programs as useless, as the kind of solid, definitive information I needed was not part of their script; the beepings and flashings of electronic equipment were, for me, a dubious indication of ghost activity or the lack thereof. The investigators themselves seemed legitimate, as background material I found on the web indicated that most had had personal experiences with hauntings; one investigator who had worked with Hawes and Wilson claimed to have grown up "with red eyes in my bedroom at night." And I did learn that ghosts are believed to be found most often in cemeteries because in earlier times people were buried in the family plot, which would be very near the house where they most likely died. Rhode Island, where the Atlantic Paranormal Society is based, is said to have 3,300 cemeteries, mostly private burial grounds used by rural families in colonial times.

Then, on an October Saturday when my husband and I were enjoying the autumn color at our house in the country, he drew my attention to an article in the local newspaper, the *Athol Daily News*. Jeff Belanger, writer and researcher for *Ghost Adventures*, was to give a pre-Halloween lecture at the public library, and his presentation would include "compelling audio and visual paranormal evidence."

The following Tuesday evening, I joined an audience that ranged from teenagers to senior citizens in the library's auditorium, a two-story space with several balconies and a large velvet-curtained stage that must have been used for films and live entertainment a century earlier. Jeff Belanger, an affable-seeming young man dressed in black T-shirt and jeans, had set up the kind of portable screen and projector I recalled from elementary school. A tape recorder was providing a soundtrack of pop music—I recognized Michael Jackson's "Thriller"—while people chose seats among the several rows of folding chairs.

The whole setup was remarkably low-tech. Belanger's talk proved a pallid version of the programs I'd seen on TV, mostly retellings of old cases and descriptions of the methods and equipment the operatives used to detect ghosts: temperature and humidity meters; a device that detects electromagnetic fields; audio recorders; and cameras that capture images in very low light. Belanger himself had never seen or communicated with a ghost—"I'm as psychic as a fence post," he confessed at one point—but he claimed to have had some kind of spirit experience while exploring the sewers of Paris, a tour that included tunnels lined with bones from ancient tombs. Judging from the comments of some ladies sitting near me, I was not the only one to leave the lecture disappointed.

This effort seemed wasted, as all I'd learned was how to use certain specialized devices, if I were so inclined, to pinpoint the location in our house where a ghost might be hovering. Clearly the ghost could, after I'd cornered it, decide to hover elsewhere. And given the age of our house and its tangled electrical wiring, other sorts of wayward energy could prompt a meter's needle to jump.

I was inclined to dismiss televised ghost hunting, as it seemed to be a case of all wind, no rain, as the investigators whipped up anticipation with their running commentary and flickering shadows produced by their own flashlights. Nothing happened in the episodes I watched, and the exercise of watching was as boring as watching paint dry, or grass grow, except that paint eventually dries and grass eventually grows.

Then I received an email from a friend who knew of my research and thought I'd like to see a blog post by Adam Curtis titled "The Ghosts in the Living Room." Curtis, an English filmmaker, had written a long, thoughtful piece about the changing nature of reality in television as demonstrated by the evolution of ghost-related programming. His article, appearing in a December 2011 blog, included archival footage from old BBC documentaries on haunted houses.[1] For me, this forty-year-old footage was a bonanza.

The earliest program shown was a 1973 interview with a young couple living in a council house (Britain's version of public housing, often suburban developments built for working-class people) in the English town of Swindon. The key focal point—the evidence of haunting—was their baby's pacifier, which would mysteriously disappear and then reappear, moving from the upstairs crib to a downstairs sterilizer, or from the stroller to the kitchen, without their knowing how. In addition, the oven would turn off by itself, and on one occasion the back door handle had started to turn and then the door began to open while the young wife watched, terrified; she had rushed to slam it closed, then stood with her back to it, crying, until her husband returned home. The young husband claimed that he often felt someone watching him. This material was heartening because it seemed more akin to my own experience.

These two people seemed entirely innocent, hapless victims of random paranormal interference in their simple home life. With chin-length brown hair and a full mustache, the husband looked like George Harrison's younger brother; his wife had a bouffant hairdo and wore a daisy-print A-line dress much like the retro-inspired spring frocks in my latest issue of *Vogue*. They appeared confused, frightened, and worried, and had decided to seek help from their pastor. The program ended with a young minister and a much older priest entering their house with a vessel of holy water. These two members of the clergy proceeded to move through the premises, flicking drops of water while the older man prayed aloud: "Peace, purity, and love reign in this home." "May the attacks of evil spirits be repelled." "Depart to the place appointed to you." Periodically the camera returned to the faces of the young couple, who remained seated as they watched, transfixed, throughout the ritual.

My immediate response was, "The British do this soooo much better!" While the alleged events were mundane, and there was scant evidence of ghost activity (one could attribute most of it to a fanciful or forgetful young mother), the effect on me, the viewer, was of having experienced a real drama with characters, setting, and a narrative with tension and closure. The setting itself was a home, not an institution or public space, as were the settings in so many of the current US versions, which featured deserted hospitals, jails, hotels, and the like. The victims were real people, with their copious seventies hair and bland, government-built flat; the young priest who came to help them seemed awkward and self-conscious in the company of his older colleague. Whether or not the exorcism worked, or even if there were a need for it, the expressions on the victims' rapt faces implied absolute faith in a positive outcome.

According to Curtis, in the mid-1970s, suburban hauntings in England increased, along with television coverage. Reporters began to use special cameras and audio equipment. One 1975 program featured an apartment block built over an old coal mine, where residents were constantly disturbed by strange noises in their flats. During a segment filmed in a bedroom, one tenant described how he had been watching television and heard a loud crashing noise from upstairs. Dressed for his television appearance in a floral print shirt and wide polka-dot tie, he showed the reporter how he'd found the contents of his golf bag scattered about: an iron on the bed, a wood halfway out the door, balls under the bed. The most remarkable thing about the episode turned out to be the man's costume, as cameras set up for eight hours recorded nothing unusual in the apartment. A technician posited that the noises were the result of the building's site and construction materials, which greatly amplified sound; he did not offer any theory regarding the golf club mayhem.

Much more conclusive, as well as entertaining, was a program filmed in another council house, where a family with four children, the Robertsons, was moving out because they were too terrified to stay. Mr. Robertson reported that when they first moved in, he thought he saw a male figure at the top of the stairs, but it had vanished almost immediately, and he'd thought nothing of it. Subsequent activity occurred in one of the upstairs bedrooms, where the youngest child, a girl, would wake up every night crying, frightened by a boy who was standing by the side of her bed. A brother took her place in the bedroom, and he proceeded to wake up screaming, "Get it out! Get it out!" When the oldest son was moved in, he experienced the bedclothes lifting and someone getting into bed with him. Mrs. Robertson had been in the middle of making her own bed when the coverlet was ripped out of her hands and thrown into a corner. The last straw was when she and one of her sons were standing in the doorway of his room and watched all the covers on his bed suddenly roll down to the bottom of the bed and then roll up again. "He was frothing at the mouth with shock," was how Mrs. Robertson described her child's reaction.

There was a backstory. A young man had been jilted by his wife and, heartbroken, returned to live here with his parents. He had moped about until one night he was talked into attending a dance; on the way home he died in a car accident. His father claimed afterward to hear his dead son moving about in his bedroom. Later the parents moved out, and, knowing nothing of the prior tenants, the Robertson family moved in.

The Robertsons also commissioned an exorcism. While things calmed down for a while, Mr. Robertson described how one night the dog crouched down and began to growl, and no one could make him stop. "It's back!" cried one of the children, and at this point the family fled the house. They moved out for good without taking any of the furniture, Mrs. Robertson feeling that even the beds might be possessed.

All of this was reported, not shown, without even a shot of the violated bedclothes or trembling children. For me, what gave the story weight was the imposing aspect of the two adults, who reminded me of characters in a Pinter play. Mr. Robertson seemed a big man, not fat but substantial under his topcoat and office clothes, with thick dark hair and sideburns and heavy eyebrows. He spoke briefly, being either reserved or resigned, I couldn't tell, but one felt a tension beneath his stoicism. His wife, with carefully curled, ash blond hair, did most of the talking, somehow managing to be shrill without raising her voice. Despite her claims of being terrified, she seemed more affronted than scared, determined to leave a situation that she couldn't control and didn't seem to want to understand.

Up until now the BBC programs had revealed little about any efforts to get at the essence of the haunting problem, which was the ghosts themselves. No psychics, mediums, or investigators seemed to be involved, only those priests who might manage to get rid of them. While engrossing and mostly believable, the victims were the feature, not the professionals brought in to interview them. This actually made for more compelling viewing, I thought, given that the spirits on programs like *Ghost Hunters* never appeared or talked or revealed what the problem might look like from their point of view; beleaguered homeowners were given only perfunctory air time at the show's start and then dismissed so that the investigators could set up their equipment, turn out the lights, and go to work. The BBC's featured victims, on the other hand, had distinct personalities, period hairdos and clothing, quirky taste in wallpaper, and real stories to tell. Further, these stories were taken at face value, not chipped away at by investigators looking for faulty radiator pipes.

Then, according to Curtis, everything changed in 1977 when the BBC introduced a psychic investigator into a family home. Extreme poltergeist activity had been reported at a house in North London, where a forty-four-year-old divorced woman lived with her four children, two boys and two girls. The next-door neighbor named Vic, a close family friend, had been summoned for help by the frightened homeowner; he described loud noises and flying objects. On one occasion a Lego had flown at him with such force that it had, despite its small size, raised a knot on his elbow. Policemen called to investigate knockings behind the wall were actually present during a poltergeist event, when an unoccupied chair moved partway across the room. At a subsequent interview, one of two poker-faced officers described how the chair had lifted slightly off the ground and moved about four feet. The officer, thinking the floor must be slanted, set a marble down on the carpet, but it did not move. Examining the chair itself, the officer did not find any wires or mechanisms attached to the chair.

This became known as the "Enfield Haunting" and provided the basis for the most elaborate of the BBC's paranormal productions, not one but a series of episodes in which the setting was enhanced artificially. Eerie music wafted in the background, and straightforward shots of the family were interspersed with views shot in a way that gave a dim, seedy creepiness to parts of the interior.

A psychic investigator, Maurice Grosse, was recruited, hopefully to enlighten the family, and the viewers, about the nature of what they had been experiencing. A retired electrical engineer and inventor, Grosse worked with the Society for Psychical Research (the same organization founded in the late 1800s) to determine whether or not there were scientific explanations for various paranormal phenomena. Grosse looked a bit like Groucho Marx, as he had chosen to offset his bald head with thick sideburns and a bushy handlebar mustache; he also wore large, black-rimmed glasses.

Once Grosse became involved, the poltergeist activity seemed to accelerate. He became the target of a flying shoe, and was present when a small settee was lifted by an unseen hand and turned upside down. Much of his time was spent in the bedroom of the two girls—eleven-year-old Janet and thirteen-year-old Rose—where furniture and other items had been moved, and knocking noises were often heard. Professing a belief that this was the most remarkable instance of poltergeist activity ever observed, Grosse decided to work with the knockings, asking the spirit to signal a "yes" or "no" to his queries with one or two knocks. Eventually Grosse was able to deduce that a man had died in the house many years earlier. He then began exhorting the ghost to leave, saying "You must leave!" and "You must stop bothering this family" and so on, but the poltergeist continued to make noise and move household objects.

During the filming, the neighbor Vic, a burly man with dark hair who wore a red plaid shirt, blue jeans, and a wide belt with a cowboy-type buckle, listed the range of events the family had experienced, and claimed that his nerves were shot. His wife, Peggy, who also had witnessed some of the unusual activity, had cropped dark hair, precisely drawn eyebrows, and hooped earrings; she seemed a no-nonsense type like Mrs. Robertson, more annoyed than afraid. Several relatives were interviewed also, testifying to witnessing various events themselves.

This program was encouraging. While none of the poltergeist activity occurred on the screen, there had been so many witnesses, including two police officers, that I felt at least some of the events described had to have happened. And the sliding chair and upturned settee could not have been caused by faulty wiring or shoddy construction. The house was old, and it had a history. While our own ghost did not throw furniture or pound on the walls, it was potentially as real as the Enfield ghost appeared to be.

But then things got muddy. The BBC revisited the family two years later, focusing on the two daughters. Curtis included a segment during which Rose and Janet are interviewed. The Enfield ghost had begun to speak in voices through Janet, a raspy, gruff male voice coming from her half-open mouth. Janet claimed that the voices came from the back of her neck, that she would have the sense of a person being behind her, and that there were several of them, whom she referred to as "Dirty Dick," "Stewart," and "Gardner." Janet did a lot of self-conscious giggling and squirming during the interview, while her sister sat quietly, with only an occasional smirk. Detractors made the obvious charge of ventriloquism, but Grosse insisted that the voices would emanate from Janet for hours, and no one could keep that up without losing their own voice.

Curtis included a still photograph from the program, in which the two girls are shown sitting side by side, laughing, with expressions that could be interpreted as conspiratorial. Later they confessed to having faked some of the things that happened in their bedroom, wanting to tease Grosse. I couldn't help but remember the Fox sisters, who had begun hearing—or effecting—mysterious tapping at about the same age.

There was more to the story. Curtis wrote that Maurice Grosse was "a wonderful man," who genuinely believed in his work and who made it his second career to visit bereaved families and confirm their belief that lost loved ones were indeed communicating. But Grosse's twenty-two-year-old daughter had died in 1976, and soon after her death, he had begun working with the Society for Psychical Research. In an autobiographical film Grosse made about his paranormal work, "it becomes clear," writes Curtis, "that Grosse believes that it is these intense feelings that give people, and the places they live in, the power to summon up poltergeists."

Curtis's piece is really about the evolving nature of televised "reality"—how fact and fiction can be blurred, how the use of documentary techniques and real people implies a reality that isn't necessarily real. Yet the initial Enfield incidents seemed genuine to me, despite the contrived sound and lighting effects and the collapsing of time so that the frequency of events was exaggerated. I have to credit the various eyewitnesses: family members, neighbors, police officers. This is hard evidence. Or is it? Is it one or two weird things happening, prompting an emotional credulity that eases the way for belief in a whole lot more? Or, in Grosse's case, is it unbearable grief that spawns a need to believe? The "Enfield Haunting," in the end, seemed like one of those murder cases in which much of the evidence is circumstantial, and in the absence of what qualifies as "definitive proof," of the sort now provided by DNA, we are left with decisions based on lack of "reasonable doubt."

While I myself wondered about much of what happened in the Enfield house, there was that initial flying Lego and the upturned settee, which, just like my hairbrush, were not set in motion by any visible hand. If this isn't definitive proof, what is?

CHAPTER SIX

❖

MY BRIEF CAREER
AS A GHOST BUSTER

While much of my armchair and library research was useful, it really was only background, context for my investigation, and I wasn't getting any closer to unraveling the mystery of my own ghost. What I wanted was a primary source, a credible person not regularly involved in the paranormal field, someone who had had inexplicable experiences similar to mine, who would be nonjudgmental, and who might have firsthand knowledge to share.

This person appeared soon after my viewing the Enfield material. I was on my way to the library one Saturday morning when I ran into a former babysitter, Kate. I hadn't seen Kate in ages, even though her parents lived next door. She had lived with us for a year when she was not attending college. One of the most self-assured and competent young people I've ever met, Kate started an extremely profitable dog-walking business while a teenager, took herself unescorted to her high school senior prom, and, after several years at a prestigious midwestern college, left to begin training as a chef. While living with us, Kate had been the lunchtime sous chef in the kitchen of one of Boston's best restaurants and now, she told me excitedly, she was designing the menu for a new bistro.

As we stood chatting on the sidewalk, I told her about how, when our male friend had expressed a belief in ghosts, Laura and Elizabeth had opened up, both describing a range of odd noises in their rooms, and Elizabeth telling us how a hair band had been thrown on her pillow in the middle of the night. "Did you experience any of this kind of thing when you were living with us?" I asked.

Kate rolled her eyes. "Ghosts? Are you kidding? There must be an army of them. Most of the time they only bothered Laura, but some nights their coming and going made so much racket it kept us all awake!"

And then she darted off, claiming to be late for work. Well, I reflected, here was a whole new can of worms. We had not just the occasional random moving of beds but constant ghost activity, indicating a prolonged encampment. Further, much of the supposedly ghost-generated noise seemed to take place in Laura's room, and she had been mostly silent on the subject. It seemed totally inconsistent with Kate's personality, but was she pulling my leg?

Whether or not Echo Bodine and her colleagues could see ghosts, after talking with Kate, I decided I could use their techniques, or a simplified version, to do a bit of investigating on my own. One night when my husband was snoring so loudly I couldn't sleep, instead of giving him the usual shove on the shoulder, I decided to change beds. Taking my pillow with me, I inched out of bed and tiptoed out the door and up the stairs to Laura's bedroom. Without turning on the light, I pushed aside the heap of pillows and stuffed animals and slid between the rather chilly sheets.

It was a particularly windy night, and tree branches seemed to be scraping against the windows, although I couldn't think how, since the magnolia we'd planted several years earlier barely reached the second floor. Laura's bedroom, which had served as a nursery for the families preceding ours, was on the fourth floor, one level below the former servants' quarters on the top floor. Her long, narrow bathroom ran along one wall of the building's air shaft, and had three large windows of thick-ribbed glass that admitted light and a cloudy view of the air shaft's soot-streaked walls and pipes. These windows also admitted sound, I soon discovered, as I could hear the vent flaps slapping and the pulley chains smacking against the metal window frames. Inside the room, small bits of something—chunks of old mortar, bits of petrified soot—rattled down the chimney from time to time, landing on the slate hearth of a fireplace that was strictly decorative, as we had removed the fake logs and gas-fed fire apparatus years earlier.

There was also a strange whining sound, the sort of noise wind can make, not the whooshing of gusts but the humming of a strong, steady passage of air along the edges of buildings. During a recent nor'easter, it had been the most disagreeable feature of the storm, the constant whistling of an abnormally high wind. This noise was softer but just as constant, and while I attributed it to some effect resulting from the proximity of a wide copper gutter that jutted out just above Laura's two bedroom windows, the sound was both eerie and unpleasant.

This was the noisiest bedroom I'd ever been in. How could our older daughter, who had occupied this room with its dainty Laura Ashley wallpaper since the age of two, ever have managed to sleep? She occasionally complained about street noise—sirens, motorcycles, the high-pitched yapping of a neighbor's dog—but this cacophony of low, persistent sounds was, in my view, a far worse irritant, as grating as the daytime whistling of a mason who had been repointing the building adjoining ours; he whistled from the time he arrived until he climbed down off the scaffolding eight hours later. After twenty minutes I took my pillow and retreated, tiptoeing back to my own bed.

If I'd remained in Laura's room—staying awake wouldn't have been difficult—would anything have happened? It was well after midnight. Might I have heard voices or seen a wispy apparition? Would our house's original owner, old Dr. Putnam, have materialized in some way? Or a child in Victorian dress? Nonsense, I told myself, all the noises I'd heard were attributable to weather. And it was dark, the middle of the night, when one's imagination can run riot and the unremarkable and ordinary begin to seem unfamiliar and strange.

I resolved to spend an entire night in Laura's room, ideally when Don had gone to bed early and I wouldn't have to explain what I was doing. If the sounds I'd heard persisted on a windless night, I would have to think seriously about contacting a medium. In the meantime I could pretend to be Echo Bodine and walk around the house testing for cold spots, alleged to indicate the presence of an energy-deprived ghost.

On a bright winter day several weeks later, with sunshine pouring in the skylight and windows, I climbed to the fourth floor and walked slowly around, circling Laura's and Elizabeth's rooms, as well as the two smaller unoccupied bedrooms. I felt nothing. Next I proceeded to the top floor, site of mysteriously banging doors, where we had knocked down most of the walls that once partitioned the space into the six small rooms where female servants slept. One half of the renovated fifth floor had become a twenty-five-foot-long room with a giant TV and wall-to-wall carpet, now stained and worn from years of the girls' birthday parties and sleepovers. Once again I walked about, going especially slowly along the edges, since I had an idea that ghosts, like cobwebs, were most likely to gather in corners. Nothing.

This foray into paranormal investigation was disheartening, and something about the clear bright light in the house that day made my activity seem not only futile but silly. Most of what I read indicated that, while spirits came at whatever time they were summoned, ghosts were most likely to be encountered at night. Yet many of the incidents in our house had occurred during the day: the disappearing hairbrush (early morning), the laundry folding (between nine in the morning and six in the evening), Dan's being pushed on the stairs (noontime).

If a ghost was up and about, I should have felt something. But maybe not. Perhaps it was lingering in some spot I'd missed, or it saw what I was up to and actively evaded me. Perhaps I just wasn't suited to ghost detection, didn't have the required perceptual abilities. Like much else in the paranormal world, it seemed, my investigation was inconclusive. Investigating ghosts was proving to be a slippery kind of research, and I began to wonder if I was destined to remain in a netherworld of maybe/maybe not.

Fortunately, the *Ghost Club Journal*, which now arrived from the United Kingdom every three months, was proving a welcome source of solid, useful information. A rather homemade-looking booklet that appeared to be produced with a copy machine and a stapler, the journal's cover, with its tall Gothic lettering and cover photo of some allegedly haunted site, was deceiving. Inside I found a broad range of useful content, including a thoughtful letter from the club's chairman, barrister Alan Murdie; "Ghosts in the News" (brief accounts of recent paranormal incidents); longer pieces on paranormal-related research, club-sponsored investigations, and guest lectures; and one or two book reviews.

The editorial stance was objective and inclusive of all points of view regarding ghosts.

A recent issue, for example, aired the theories of skeptic Vic Tandy. Tandy, an electrical engineer, posited that infrasound—imperceptible sound vibrations resulting from various external sources—could cause feelings of anxiety, fear, and nausea, as well as a sense of another's presence, even the notion that one was seeing apparitions. Such vibrations can be caused by weather, jet streams, passing vehicles, or machinery.

For me, Tandy's infrasound data questioned much of what the TV ghost hunters tended to regard as evidence of paranormal activity. Imperceptible sound vibrations, added to weather and temperature changes, could account for much of the data generated by their equipment. But his theory could not, in my opinion, account for the presence I felt in the bedroom and when practicing the piano, as the presence was consistent in being felt only in the early morning or at the piano and did not waver with the weather or the level of traffic outside our house. While Tandy's work did seem to negate much of what passed for paranormal, it still left space—albeit a smaller one—for ghosts.

CHAPTER SEVEN

STYMIED BY CONFUSION, EMBARRASSMENT, AND INDIGNATION

This was the point at which I might have sought professional help, but I wasn't ready to contact a medium. I was much more comfortable poking around the edges of the paranormal, reading about the colorful experiences of people like Echo Bodine, and making cursory searches of my own house in the bright light of day. Spending just a half hour in Laura's bedroom had scared me off nighttime explorations. I knew I should repeat that experiment, but I kept putting it off.

Clearly a more efficient course would be to hire Bodine or one of her colleagues and have them cruise around the upstairs bedrooms. But I needed more clarity about what I might be getting myself into, and I didn't want to bring a stranger into my home, someone who might or might not offer reliable information about who was "haunting" us. It seemed like overkill. Our ghost didn't scare us by appearing bedside in the middle of the night or keep us awake by rapping on the walls. Its appearances were widely spaced, often many months apart, and who knew if the ghost would even show up for Bodine's visit?

Besides, I was enjoying the process, exploring the paranormal world and learning what kinds of people had lived and raised families in our home. I was also, admittedly, keeping at arm's length any definitive identification. A nameless ghost was one thing; a specific person, however invisible, was something else. Blasé as I had been about having a ghost, there is a creepiness factor to knowing "it" is really a "he" or a "she."

I was less satisfied with what my exploration had yielded in the way of usable information. By this point I had read volumes and spent many hours watching TV. I'd become so immersed in the research itself that I felt a need to look up and ask myself, what should I believe? Echo Bodine claims to see and speak with ghosts, and perhaps she can; if so, then ghosts must exist. And certainly the Enfield saga provided undeniable evidence of paranormal activity. Why was I feeling ambivalent?

I was hardly getting reinforcement for a pro-ghost point of view from friends and acquaintances, and I am guilty of being susceptible to the beliefs, and scorn, of others. Yes, I say, we very well may have a ghost, look what's happened! But then I encounter someone who is aghast at my project, usually a man, like the colleague who was unequivocal in his disbelief that I would even entertain the idea that ghosts exist. Many of the men I've told about my ghost research are not only disbelieving but almost annoyed that I should even broach the subject; women, though often initially skeptical, tend to be less harsh in their denials, and if pushed a bit, interested. Some even have their own ghost stories to tell, like a neighbor who told me that she has seen a man in her den; he wears a Civil War–era uniform and seems preoccupied with her books. I have found, however, that I am unable to risk censure or ridicule if I reveal the nature of my research, so whenever I am in a public place such as in the library or on the subway, I reflexively cover any reading material that says "Ghost," or "Haunted," in large letters.

One morning I came across a *New York Times* front-page article about a Dr. Daryl Bem, an emeritus faculty member in the Psychology Department at Cornell and, according to the newspaper, one of the most prominent research psychologists of his generation. Dr. Bem had published a paper documenting the existence of extrasensory perception, which cited studies of more than a thousand subjects over a ten-year period; he was being excoriated by his colleagues, who referred to his work as "a joke" and "an embarrassment." As I read on, increasingly indignant on behalf of Dr. Bem, I had to conclude that there was bias, if not outright hostility, on the part of Bem's peers. His detractors claimed faulty methodology, skewed data, selective sampling, whatever they could think of to discredit his results.[1] (Dr. Bem would later appear as a guest on *The Colbert Report*, mainly because one of his experiments asked students to perceive hidden pornographic images, and Stephen Colbert had great fun with "extrapornception.")

A factor muddying documentation of paranormal phenomena is, as I was discovering, a deep rift within the scientific community: those scientists like Bem who study phenomena linked to the paranormal are often regarded as pariahs, their field of study irrelevant at best. Being able to communicate telepathically, using only the mind, has been regarded as an indicator that some part of our being exists outside the physical body, not connected to the brain or sensory organs, and it is this aspect—this soul or spirit or sixth sense—that believers in the ineffable cling to as proof that some part of us may live on after death. It is also an idea that gives most scientists fits, as they prefer to attribute all our functions to the physical body, that is, the five sensory organs plus the brain.

Since ghosts are supposed to be the spirits of nonliving people, they fall into the paranormal realm, a realm that is called "parapsychology" if one is a scientist working in a psychology department. This is a realm considered off-limits by most of the scientific community. And those scientists working in parapsychology are far outnumbered, leaving any significant findings about previously unidentified human abilities discredited, forgotten, or both.

Most significant in this respect was a Dr. J. B. Rhine, who spent fifty years conducting experiments to prove that we have telepathic powers. Rhine and his superior at Harvard Medical School, William McDougall, founded the Parapsychology Laboratory at Duke University in 1927, intending to use scientific methodology to prove psychic phenomena, specifically extrasensory perception. Despite his prominence as a researcher, what Rhine may or may not have proved was buried after his death beneath layers of contradictory persiflage created by his scientific colleagues.

I read about Rhine's work in *Unbelievable: Investigations into Ghosts, Poltergeists, Telepathy, and Other Unseen Phenomena, from the Duke Parapsychology Laboratory,* by Stacy Horn.[2] Rhine was a brilliant and charismatic man who was determined to prove afterlife by validating ESP. His experiments mostly involved having subjects identify images they couldn't see, symbols that were printed on one side of a set of cards. This was his modus operandi, and he stuck to it, obsessively, claiming that certain subjects could identify the hidden images consistently, thus proving human capacity for telepathy.

For me, all this was beside the point. I wanted to support Rhine's effort, but I could not see the connection between knowing what was on a card and the existence of ghosts, or afterlife; Rhine's and others' claim that there was a direct connection—that the human facility for seeing, hearing, or knowing something most people didn't was evidence of human immortality—made no sense to me. Only some people seemed to have this ability, for one thing, and their ability to know what others did not could be an individual talent, a feature of the mind that hasn't yet been identified. This was confusing, and I felt I must be missing something, but the more I thought about it, the more I decided that there really wasn't much of a connection. "Extrasensory" was more "supersensory," indicating an ability to see, hear, smell, and so on, more than the average person—that is, to see a figure or to hear a voice invisible or inaudible to most humans—and even this ability didn't seem so remarkable. Dogs can hear and smell things we humans cannot, and communicate with one another by peeing and sniffing, a fact I can attest to because I have spent many hours on the end of a leash while our dog Alice reads her "p-mails." Telepathy, though, goes a step further, as it describes an ability to communicate without spoken or written language. This, again, may be a feature of the mind that is as yet undeveloped in most of us. However, if a medium really possesses this "extra" sense of telepathy, and is able to have a two-way conversation with the dead, *that* is proof of afterlife (the proof, incidentally, being provided by the talking dead).

Hoping for clarity, even if it were clarity based on fiction, I went to see Clint Eastwood's movie *Hereafter*, in which Matt Damon plays an unwilling psychic plagued by those wanting him to contact their departed friends and relatives. He has fled to London to avoid the many people clamoring to pay him for his services. I was curious to see how Eastwood, known for his macho roles and sensibility, would treat the paranormal. Respectfully, as it turned out, and I wondered if concerns with his own mortality (he was born in 1930) hadn't prompted an interest in a narrative built upon the possibility of life after death.

Early in the movie, the character Damon plays is convinced by a bereaved young woman who has lost a little brother to do his psychic thing. Once he holds her hands, makes physical contact, Damon begins to receive messages from her recently departed loved one. It was as though he were waiting to talk and only needed Damon, with his psychic ability, to pick up the phone.

Or, as a friend suggested, was it not the dead child, but the information that was "out there," and all Damon did was access it? Which suggests that information about everything that ever happened is "out there," and the dead have nothing to do with it.

Perhaps. And eventually I may have to accept that mysterious forces other than ghosts are responsible for the events in our house. What is really interesting, and far more relevant to me, are the stories and events that Dr. Rhine did not study, events brought to his attention by members of the public who wanted his input on a range of inexplicable incidents: beds rising off the floor and shaking, water barrels filling themselves, houses where china and lamps and bottles of bleach flew about as if driven by a mini tornado. During her examination of Rhine's archives, Stacy Horn, the author of *Unbelievable*, found dozens of these stories, as Rhine, whose research and alleged results made him a celebrity, was bombarded with accounts of bizarre experiences and requests for professional guidance. Horn actually seemed more interested in these events than in Rhine's experiments, as she devotes many pages to the paranormal occurrences described in letters to Dr. Rhine and even includes her own extraordinary ghost story.

When she was about seven years old, Horn was wandering around her neighborhood and got lost. She passed by a yard where an elderly woman was playing with several cats, and as she loved cats, Horn asked if she could pet them. Afterward the woman invited her into her house, served her milk and cookies, and then walked her home. A year later the author decided to revisit the lady and her cats, but when she made her way to the house, she found it deserted, the yard overgrown and the roof collapsed. She stood there, "totally flummoxed," until a woman from the house next door appeared and asked if she could help her. When the young Stacy asked what happened to the old lady and her cats, she was told, "No one has lived here for a very long time." "I knew that she was telling me that the lady was dead and that she was dead before I had met her," Horn writes. Nonetheless, she entered the long-abandoned house and was told by a voice, "like someone was talking very quietly, right beside me," to go into the bedroom. She did and found a carton with four kittens in it. Horn picked up the box and took the kittens home. "The kittens were a present from the old lady, I decided."[3]

Horn reflects that, as a child, she was unfazed by the experience because at that age she was taking everything in, simply trying to understand the world, and that this particular experience made her receptive to the idea of ghosts and the paranormal, concluding, "What's so scary about ghosts if they lead you to kittens?"[4]

This is the kind of story that raises so many intriguing questions—the old lady must have been a ghost, but how did she arrange Horn's experience? Was time travel involved? Why did she choose Horn, or did Horn somehow choose her? In trying to interpret this complex, multifaceted example, findings about ESP don't get you very far.

Poking around the internet for stories that might echo Horn's memory of a childhood experience, I came across a new and very professional-looking website for *Ghost Hunters*, the television series now an adjunct to the Atlantic Paranormal Society, an expanded version of the two plumbers' original ghost-busting partnership.

The programs I had watched had been reruns of much earlier episodes, something I didn't realize. The more recent *Ghost Hunter* programs had an enlarged crew of investigators, which now included Jim Hawes's daughter. Hawes himself was looking and talking much more like a television star than a plumber: tanned, his head shaved, and extremely comfortable in front of the camera. He professed a determination to help people who were troubled by paranormal events, "help" taking the form of identifying a non-paranormal explanation (it's just defective pipes) or by confirming what the client had heard or seen ("You're not crazy, our equipment picked up evidence of spirit activity").

At a 1950s-era house in Tomkinsville, Kentucky, for example, a family had begun seeing both a male and a female figure; they heard sounds of someone walking around and at night saw flickering shadows. The family believed that their renovations had upset the former owners, who had returned to haunt them. Hawes and his crew went to work, deploying cameras and detectors and, after spending the night inside the house, determined that the pipes from an ice machine were making the sounds resembling footsteps, and flickering shadows resulted from car lights on a nearby highway. But according to the vibration detector, the presence of spirits was quite likely.

While I preferred cases set in normal family houses like my own, I couldn't resist watching an episode featuring Hammond Castle, located just north of Boston in Gloucester, Massachusetts. In my early twenties I had been to a dance there, and I remembered its grand, medieval-style rooms, and distinctly 1930s powder room, like two layers of history at once. Technically Hammond Castle was a private house, as it had been built by a brilliant but rather eccentric inventor, John Hammond Jr. Hammond was an electrical engineer who had been mentored by Thomas Edison and who had four hundred patents to his name, among them the basis for the remote control. The castle is now a museum, and the *Ghost Hunters* team had been summoned by the director, John Pettibone. Figures of a man and a woman had been sighted on the balcony overlooking the great hall by a group of Girl Scouts. In the past, visitors had heard voices in the library, and on several occasions books had flown off the shelves. And on a large bed in the medieval bedroom, which was roped off, an apparition of a woman had been seen and the bedclothes disturbed.

The Hammonds themselves had believed in the paranormal. Mrs. Hammond was an astrologer and psychic, and séances were held at the castle. One of the artifacts remaining from these days was a Farraday cage, a wire-enclosed capsule-shaped chamber large enough to hold a standing adult. (*Farraday cage*, I later learned, was the generic term for enclosures made of material that blocks static and nonstatic electrical fields; now sold in the form of bags, these devices are most often used to protect electronics. Structures such as the one owned by the Hammonds were used to isolate mediums from man-made radio waves.)

Hawes took a startlingly direct approach, figuring that if the Hammonds' spirits were in the castle, they would understand what he was doing and be more than willing to participate. Standing in the great hall, he looked up and addressed the Hammonds by name, saying, "Can you say something or make a sound to let us know you are here?" Hawes continued, "We are not psychic and we need you to be aggressive in communication." Detecting equipment was placed in various parts of the castle. "We are using techniques that the Hammonds would have understood and approved of," he explained to onlookers.

A range of devices was placed in the medieval bedroom on top of the six-hundred-year- old bed, where the bedclothes had been disturbed. The results were remarkable, the most striking manifestation of possible ghost activity I'd seen on television. As Hawes began asking questions, one device, a geophone, which was the size and shape of a cigarette pack, began to flash on and off. A sprightly dialogue ensued, each of Hawes's questions eliciting an immediate response in the form of one or two flashes: "Is it you, Mrs. Hammond? Are you here? Are you in the bed? Were you the owner of the bed? Are you trying to communicate?" Later the investigators returned to the bedroom and asked additional questions, which elicited more flashes. "I'm goose-bumped out!" one investigator gasped.

Then, toward the end of the nighttime vigil, a chandelier in the dining room began to sway. After ascertaining that there was no effect from airflow or vibrations in the room, Hawes and his crew watched, seemingly spellbound, as the chandelier swung back and forth in increasingly wide arcs.

Despite the remarkable communication between the investigators and Mrs. Hammond via the geophone, I wondered why the Hammonds themselves didn't appear. It was they, presumably, who answered Hawes's questions. Dr. Hammond was reported to have said that, after he died, if he came back, it would be as a black cat. Perhaps he has, as black cats have been sighted on the grounds. But if anyone could rig a building for special effects, he would be the man. Did Hammond invent another, more specialized, remote control?

CHAPTER EIGHT

❁

DR. SACKS PULLS THE RUG OUT, AND DR. ALEXANDER PUTS IT BACK

During the time I was immersed in ghost-hunting television programs, a review of Oliver Sacks's newest book, *Hallucinations*, appeared in the *New York Times*. Based on his own and many others' clinical experience, it was described as an examination of a range of visual and auditory experiences that, while often attributed to mental illness or injury, were in fact caused by the brain's normal functioning in abnormal situations. The onset of blindness, for example, could elicit various kinds of visions, as the brain's sensory mechanisms sought to compensate for the lack of real visual material. Religious and out-of-body experiences, apparitions, voices, visits from the departed—all could be traced, according to Sacks, to activity in the cerebral cortex. The relevance of this material to my paranormal research was obvious, and I ordered a copy.

It was a relief to be reading a book with a respectable-looking cover and no cartoonish ghost images or Gothic lettering, just a simple drawing of an eye that could have been copied from a medical text. The tales told within, however, were as bizarre as any related by Echo Bodine, as patients described visions of tiny pink men and animals, hearing sounds of people singing and arguing, feeling terror at being roused from sleep by something sitting on their chest.

What I found to be the most extraordinary example of brain-generated imagery appeared in the first chapter. Dr. Sacks had been summoned to a nursing home, where a woman in her nineties, totally blind for the past several years, had begun seeing detailed scenes of men, women, and children, in what she described as Eastern dress, in bright colors and with long draperies (saris, perhaps?), all walking up and down the stairs; sometimes she also saw animals and landscapes. The people took no notice of her but seemed quite real; they appeared randomly, like a movie being turned on and off by someone else's remote control. Was she suffering from a stroke? Alzheimer's? Dementia?

Sacks was able to reassure the old lady—and her caretakers— that she was not losing her mind, as she had feared. Instead she was suffering from Charles Bonnet syndrome, a condition identified by a Swiss naturalist in the mid-1700s. Bonnet, whose father was blind and who would later become blind himself, believed that, despite the loss of sight, visual parts of the brain remained active and relied on memory for a source of imagery from which it fabricated something for the blind person to see.

While I was astonished to learn that the human brain was capable of generating such complex and varied imagery on its own, like a television compensating for satellite failure by recy-cling its own selection of prerecorded programs, I was more surprised that the medical community had only recently grasped how common this affliction is. The problem, it seemed, was lack of documentation, since most people, the elderly in particular, were unwilling to describe their hallucinations, not wanting to be thought demented, particularly since much hallucinated material consists of images that are grotesque and distorted. Sacks credited new techniques of brain imaging and monitoring that "have allowed us to define which parts of the brain are responsible for different sorts of hallucinations."[1]

And one did not have to be blind to hallucinate, to have involuntary visions that seemed totally real but could not be perceived by anyone else. Such experiences could be caused by extended isolation, sleep deprivation, bereavement, migraine headaches, and epilepsy.

Many of Sacks's case histories described phenomena also claimed by those working within the paranormal context: seemingly inexplicable sounds, light effects, briefly glimpsed figures and faces, even odors. I recalled all the alleged evidence of hauntings I'd seen on television, the shadows and the orbs of light, the strange gray-haired lady glimpsed by a guest at a birthday party, the male figure that Mr. Robertson saw at the top of the stairs. For Sacks these were all versions of the same thing, that is, a person sensing things that no one else did and that were not there, due to their particular physical or mental situation, or both. The hallucinatory experience itself ranged from the amorphous aura of the migraine sufferer to the elaborate, fantastical productions described by several of Sacks's patients with Charles Bonnet syndrome.

Sacks's theories, illustrated by numerous case histories, seemed to me to eliminate about three-quarters of what passed for evidence of paranormal activity. In his chapter "Narcolepsy and Night Hags," for example, Sacks described the causes and effects of sleep paralysis, which struck a familiar chord. Several months earlier, I'd been talking about ghosts with one of my daughter's college roommates, now a writer living in a Victorian-era house in Amherst, Massachusetts. The house was definitely haunted, Eliza told me, because her partner had been accosted during the night by something sitting on her chest and trying to smother her; Eliza had had to help the woman as she struggled to release herself from the invisible demon's grip. And I recalled a *Ghost Hunters* episode in which a home owner had described a similar attack, an unseen thing rendering him helpless, unable to move when he awakened.

One of Sacks's patients described the same kind of experience, telling him how her body became numb after she went to bed, and then "it was almost as if someone sat on my back, pressing me deeper into the mattress . . . [then] the thing on my back got down and laid next to me . . . I could feel it lying beside me, breathing."[2] These kinds of experiences, which typically occur during the phases of deep sleep known as REM sleep (because of rapid eye movement), are often experienced by those with narcolepsy (a disorder that prompts sudden, uncontrollable seizures of deep sleep), but single or occasional episodes have been reported among the general population (again, there might be many more reports if people weren't concerned about being thought mad). And often the paralysis is accompanied by "the sense of a malignant presence, and an overall sense of absolute helplessness and abject terror."[3]

(The word *nightmare*, Sacks pointed out, had evolved from a folkloric concept, the *mare* referring to a demonic woman who suffocated sleepers by lying on their chests.)

I thought about the young man on *Ghost Adventures* who had talked so movingly about his own childhood hauntings, and wondered if he, too, was narcoleptic or epileptic, and had, like another of Sacks's patients, from the age of five experienced a range of hallucinations: seeing an angel, hearing her name whispered, feeling and seeing ants crawling on her legs. This patient's ghost had been banished, not by exorcists or ghost busters, but by medication.

As a physician and professor of neurology with many years of clinical experience, one who cites a range of medical studies and learned colleagues, Dr. Sacks had for me a far different level of credibility from mediums who saw what I couldn't or plumbers with a bundle of detecting equipment and little in the way of demonstrable results. And Sacks, who had experimented extensively with drugs like LSD, mescaline, and morphine at an earlier stage in his life, should, I thought, know a hallucination when he saw one.

All during my research into the paranormal, I'd been recording the qualifiers as I read or watched accounts of otherworldly experiences—hints, for example, that the subject of an experience might be overly credulous, or imaginative, emotionally taxed, or even duplicitous. While I had noted implications of mental and emotional imbalance—one ghost hunter had attempted suicide, and in several cases drug use was implied—what struck me most often was a strong desire to experience spirit activity. This was most obvious among the bereaved. William James and Arthur Conan Doyle both had suffered the loss of close family members. Maurice Grosse, the Enfield investigator, had lost his daughter. The widows and mothers who flocked to early séances were desperate to make contact with the spirits of their husbands and sons.

In a chapter called "The Haunted Mind," Sacks cites a study in which a significant number of new widows claimed that they had seen, heard, even chatted with their dead spouses.[4] He describes the bereavement hallucinations of several patients—a woman returned home to be greeted by the voice of her dead husband; a young boy saw his dead father jogging past the house—commenting that "especially common are hallucinations engendered by loss and grief." But as I proceeded through Sacks's bereavement examples, I began to feel stirrings of resistance. He seemed to me to be painting every patient with the same neurological brush. A young girl, whose grandfather had died the previous winter, was spending the summer at her grandparents' house; she was seated at the kitchen table when she saw her grandfather walk in the room. "I was so glad to see him that I got up to meet him. I said, 'Grandpa,' and as I moved towards him, he suddenly wasn't there. . . . I said to my mother that I had really seen him clearly, and she said that I had seen him because I wanted to. I hadn't been consciously thinking of him and still do not understand how I could have seen him so clearly."[5]

Sacks separates the seemingly random hallucinations experienced by those with medical conditions like blindness or epilepsy from the hallucinations of those who envision scenes based on their own past experience. I was becoming aware that this represented a critical difference. People with a medical cause for hallucinations were one thing, and otherwise healthy people with a perceived need or desire to hallucinate were quite another; it seemed to me that Sacks was confidently dumping every variety of spiritual or paranormal experience into the same hallucinogenic bag. Despite or because of his qualifications, however, I reminded myself that Sacks had a point of view, and it was that point of view that he brought to every patient's story, including those stories falling within the category of religious experience: all of it was attributable to a quirk in the brain, whether involuntary or self-induced. Thus prayer and meditation could lead to a hypnotic state, where what is imagined is perceived as real, such as hearing the voice of God. Here Sacks quotes William James, who attended many séances and observed mediums who he believed were "in altered states of consciousness . . . achieved by self-hypnosis," which allowed them to have hallucinations, "whose content was shaped by the questions they were asked."[6] Sacks referred to a woman who claimed to have heard God telling her to run for office, and she proceeded to do so. He was very hard on Joan of Arc: "Joan of Arc may have had temporal lobe epilepsy with ecstatic auras," he wrote, prompting her to hear the voice of God commanding that she don armor and rout the English from France.[7] On a more pedestrian level, he added, we "all are susceptible to the powers of suggestion, especially if it is combined with emotional arousal and ambiguous stimuli."[8] That is, if we find ourselves alone in a house that is said to be haunted, once night falls and the wind blows, we are likely to see and hear things we might not otherwise.

Clearly, I reflected, Sacks's bias stemmed from his own considerable knowledge and experience, and one is inclined to credit this bias. Yet, untutored as I was in neurological science, and hence unable to assess, let alone verify, Dr. Sacks's conclusions, I found myself pulling back as I reached the end of his book. Yes, it seemed quite likely that he and his colleagues were correct in their diagnoses of many people's visions and out-of-body experiences, especially given the brain imaging equipment now available. But Sacks was mainly concerned with describing the results of the brain's functioning, not how it actually worked, and I found it hard to grasp the scientific reasoning behind his claims. Isn't it possible, I wondered, that paranormal phenomena happen, too? And possibly more often than we realize, because people with detectors and sensors aren't around to record them, and those who have paranormal experiences may not tell, fearing the same stigma of madness as those suffering from hallucinations?

One of Sacks's bereavement stories—it was similar to the

others, so I don't know why it got to me—prompted me, mentally, to dig in my heels. A man's father had died at age eighty-five after a heart operation, passing away before his son could reach the hospital. Several nights later, the son reported, "I awoke in the night. I did not feel groggy or disoriented, and my thoughts and vision were clear. I saw someone sitting on the corner of my bed. It was my dad, wearing his khaki slacks and tan polo shirt. . . . He sat there for a moment and then said—did he speak or just convey the thought?—'Everything is all right.'"[9] I wanted to argue with Sacks, to tell him that maybe this perfectly healthy, sane, and recently bereaved man may not have been subject to his brain's functioning independently, deciding on its own to provide him with a comforting hallucination. Perhaps, I wanted to insist to Sacks, he had seen his father sitting on the end of his bed because his father *was* sitting on the end of his bed.

I wouldn't know a cerebral cortex from a golf ball, and I could not refute Dr. Sacks's assessments in an informed way. But I had read enough to have my own point of view, which was that the preponderance of chemically and biologically caused visions did not necessarily disprove the existence of spirits. The paranormal or supernatural experience might also occur, albeit less often than religious leaders and psychics would have us believe.

When I was a college student, I recall one final exam that was actually fun to take. The course, an interdepartmental offering called something like Western European Mythology, encompassed pagan, Nordic, and Judeo-Christian myths, as well as witchcraft and Freudian psychology. For the final exam we were given a half-page "myth" fabricated by the instructor and asked to interpret it from three different mythological points of view.

Remembering this exam, I thought about how the various groups relevant to my personal investigation would interpret the events that had occurred in my house. Echo Bodine, I felt certain, would climb briskly to the fourth floor, do a quick turn around the bedrooms, and then draw my attention to an area in one of the rooms where she could see a young woman wearing an apron and holding a feather duster. She would proceed to engage this long-dead female in conversation, find out why she was hanging around, and then try to talk her into "moving on."

The ghost busters Hawes and Wilson, after taking down information regarding where and what inexplicable events had transpired in my house, would head for the cellar in order to begin a survey of the building's electrical and plumbing systems. Then, after setting up meters and cameras, they would spend the night prowling around the top two floors of the house, while monitoring their detecting equipment for magnetic fields and the like. At the end of their stay I would receive an evaluation and learn that I was graced with faulty wiring and bad plumbing (most likely), a residual haunting (left over energy from long-departed spirits), or an intelligent haunting (some spirit was definitely in residence).

Dr. Sacks, a self-professed atheist who eschewed the paranormal, might give Bodine the benefit of the doubt and say that she was self-hypnotized and thus able to conjure visions that seemed quite real to her and suited the situation. He would, after recording the content and frequency of my experiences, focus on the medical me, asking about recent events in my life, assessing my state of mind, and reviewing my health records. If I seemed sufficiently unhinged by an ongoing hallucinatory situation, he would probably recommend medication.

Was I becoming too credulous myself, challenging Dr. Sacks because I was increasingly invested in the idea that we really might have a ghost? I had to admit that Dr. Sacks had science—and a lot of it—on his side. As I was sitting in my office pondering the usefulness of his book to my own situation, the January issue of the *Ghost Club Journal* came sailing in through the mail slot. It was like other serendipitous events in my research, hearing the plop of a fat envelope landing on the tile floor just as I was staring at Oliver Sacks's picture on the book jacket—with his black turtleneck, tidy gray beard, and wire-rimmed spectacles propped on his forehead—and thinking that anyone who looked so kindly and who was published so often by the *New Yorker* had to be believed.

Dedicated primarily to reports on events surrounding the club's 150th anniversary, this *Ghost Club Journal* was, at thirty-nine pages, a particularly buxom issue. The cover featured a striking photograph of a Gothic façade, taken at twilight so that interior lighting emphasized the multipaned, arched windows. After skimming articles on the 150th-anniversary conference and one titled "The Ghosts of the Clyde," I turned to the Book Review section, which included Sacks's *Hallucinations* and *Proof of Heaven: A Neurosurgeon's Journey into the Afterlife*, by Dr. Eben Alexander.

The reviewer, Phillip Carr, affected an upbeat, chatty, but noncommittal tone as he summarized Sacks's book, referring to one chapter, "On the Threshold of Sleep," as being "particularly relevant to those involved in ghost investigations," as it dealt with hypnagogia, "where faces, figures, shadows, sounds, past experiences often can appear, sometimes in terrifying forms. Sacks asserts that these psychical or paranormal experiences simply have a neurological basis." Carr concluded that the book challenged many ideas about the paranormal "from a fresh perspective, which can be no bad thing."

Proof of Heaven, however, written by a neurosurgeon who claimed to have experienced heaven while in a coma, got an unqualified thumbs-up from Carr, who described it as "an inspiring, moving, even joyous book to read by comparison."[10]

Apparently many others agreed with Carr, as Dr. Alexander's book was number one on the *New York Times* combined print and e-book best-seller list when I checked later. Once again I was nudged by a timely coincidence: soon afterward, I sat in Trinity Church on Easter morning and listened to the rector, a PhD in English and former dean of the Washington Cathedral, cite *Proof of Heaven* in his sermon. While indicating some reservations about Dr. Alexander's actual experience, Reverend Lloyd was clear that the outcome—a belief in life lived according to the tenets of connection with others, in "peace and harmony"—was a salutary one. "I have to say I don't know what to make of Dr. Alexander's book. . . . In any case, it can at least encourage us to doubt our modern thoughts of what is possible, and question our close-minded skepticism." I decided to buy a copy.

Alexander's book, a slim paperback, was a skimpy affair with respect to printing and paper quality, and the very short chapters had a sort of breezy, gee-whiz, sit-down-and-listen-up-while-I-tell-you-what-happened-to-me! kind of style. Yet I had to give the author credit for the clearest descriptions of medical phenomena I'd ever read.

A Duke University–educated neurosurgeon with impressive credentials—Harvard Medical School faculty, fifteen years of surgical practice at prominent Boston hospitals—Dr. Alexander had written an account of his "NDE" (near-death experience). Alexander was in a coma for seven days after mysteriously contacting bacterial meningitis, an affliction most often fatal in adults. During his coma, he recalls passing through a sort of primal ooze and then entering heaven after traveling through a tunnel of light; he was accompanied by celestial music and "a beautiful girl with high cheekbones and deep blue eyes," wearing "peasant-like clothes" and surrounded by "millions of butterflies . . . a river of life and color." The girl conveyed a message to him, wordlessly: "You are loved and cherished." For Alexander, who felt "a vast and crazy sensation of relief," it was "the single most real experience of my life."[11]

Rejecting the scientific notion that decreased oxygen and blood flow to the brain caused hallucinations, Dr. Alexander claimed that his brain had stopped functioning altogether, rendered inactive for seven days by inflammation, and thus was incapable of generating any visual or aural imagery. He was not expected to live, let alone regain his perceptual faculties. On the eighth day Alexander woke up, opened his eyes, and commenced a remarkably brief period of recuperation, after which he was able to record and interpret what had happened while he was in a coma, his "proof of heaven."

While Sacks's book told the stories of many people, Alexander had only his own, but he buttressed his fantastical tale with extensive material on the brain and how it functions, describing what had happened to him, medically, in great detail. He also explained how the scientific community, himself included, couldn't really reconcile religious beliefs with those of science. Now he, a man of science and a nominal Episcopalian, had been transported to heaven and returned to tell about it.

Thanks to the *Ghost Club Journal*, I now had access to two opposing views of basic paranormal experience, both those of highly qualified medical people with intimate personal experience. While Dr. Sacks seemed to have pulled the rug out from under most of the furniture of the paranormal world—apparitions, disembodied voices, and so on—Dr. Alexander put it back with his compelling account of being transported to heaven and becoming part of a cosmic consciousness. While I was initially put off by Alexander's description of his experience, with its celestial music, all-encompassing love, and so forth, he did do a good job of describing what had happened to him medically, how the perceptual faculties of the brain actually work, and he finished with a compelling treatise on how science has utterly failed to address the phenomenon of consciousness. While I didn't question his scientific data, or his position regarding the myopic vision of those engaged in pure science, or even his genuine belief in the story as he told it, I did find the idea that he had been to heaven and communed with our Creator more than a bit sketchy, particularly the bit about the beautiful girl and all the butterflies, which seemed more like an illustration from a child's book of fairy tales. Perhaps Dr. Alexander had not been as brain dead as he and others thought, or maybe his near-death experience prevented the clinical detachment necessary to call a hallucination a hallucination. I had no way of knowing.

There were some qualifiers in Alexander's book, some evidence that he, too, had a pressing need to get outside himself. Born out of wedlock to teenage parents, he had been given up for adoption; in later years, when he tried to contact his birth parents, he was refused. He drank to excess when young, and in middle age, consciously acknowledging that he had been rejected twice by his biological mother and father, he entered a period of depression.

I went to the internet, hoping to find reviews of Alexander's book that might bolster my skepticism. *Scientific American*'s Michael Shermer articulated a thought I'd had myself, that experiences such as Dr. Alexander's "are called near death experiences [because] the people who have them are not actually dead."[12] In the *New York Times* I was pleased to find a quote from Dr. Martin Samuels, someone I actually knew, the father of one of my daughter's schoolmates and an extraordinarily nice guy who was now chairman of the Neurology Department at Brigham and Women's Hospital. "There is no way to know, in fact, that his neo-cortex was shut down. . . . It is an interpretation made after the fact," Marty commented. Further, "The fact that he is a neurosurgeon is no more relevant than if he was a plumber."[13]

I studied Dr. Alexander's photo, and then with the help of YouTube, I watched a segment of an interview on *The View*, the popular daytime talk show hosted by women. A handsome man with dark hair, strong features, and an earnest expression, Dr. Alexander had just a tinge of the nerd about him, despite his natty striped shirt and bow tie. While being interviewed, despite interviewer Joy Behar's blatantly skeptical tone, he was almost affectless, neither furrowing his brow nor cracking a smile. He began to remind me of the taciturn character Don Draper in the television series *Mad Men*, and I realized it was because Draper had a similar background, having been rejected by his parents, suffering from alcohol abuse, and sinking into a lethargic depression in his middle age.

Here I was again in deep scientific water, way over my head. How could I frame Dr. Alexander's claims in a way I could begin to assess? I peered at the small illustration of a brain in my American Heritage Dictionary and, remembering almost nothing from my one biology course, wondered if, once the cortex was inoperative, the areas labeled "medulla" or "thalamus" might have kicked in.

What I really wanted was to see Sacks and Alexander go at it in a debate, airing their diametrically opposed views on the existence of a separate consciousness, the existence of spiritual life. Sacks, who describes himself as "an old Jewish atheist," no doubt would diagnose his colleague as suffering from "ecstatic" seizure, a form of epileptic seizure, most famously experienced by Dostoyevsky, "that produces feelings of ecstasy or transcendent joy."

Alexander would counter that his inflamed cortex was incapable of producing visual or aural data; his travel to heaven proved that our spirits are eternal. And science has, to date, done a lousy job of accounting for the phenomenon of consciousness.

Confirming the existence of ghosts and spirits would confirm that there is life after death and go a long way toward verifying the existence of God and heaven. Working in the other direction—confirming the existence of heaven, as Dr. Alexander believed he had done—would prove that there is life after death, and more than just possibly an alternative world of spirits. It would be so convenient if I could accept what Dr. Alexander believed! But I just couldn't. I felt aligned with Dr. Sacks on this one, certain that Alexander had been hallucinating as he regained consciousness and that the beautiful girl in peasant dress, along with the butterflies, had been lifted whole cloth by his brain from some image stored long ago, most likely, I thought, as far back as childhood. And the intensity of his experience had to be due to his having had a "grand mal" seizure, similar to that suffered by Dostoyevsky, who is described in *Hallucinations* as having experienced "bliss, rapture, a sense of being transported to heaven."[14]

But Dr. Alexander's book did explain, in language I could understand, how the brain works, or is thought to work, and how "consciousness" is a much-debated concept. For most scientists, and practitioners like Dr. Sacks, consciousness is simply the living brain going about its business of seeing, feeling, thinking. For Alexander, as well as for those who subscribe to the supernatural or paranormal constructs, consciousness is the spirit, or soul, separate from the brain, the body, all that is material and thus discernible. It is the part of us that lives on after death.

Once at a cocktail party, a physicist friend told his wife and me that we were really just clumps of energy (I don't think he used the word *clump*), like everything else in the room. In his book, Alexander does an excellent job of explaining what this means, as atoms are broken down into protons and particles, so that at a very submolecular level, the component parts are all the same. I was able to grasp this notion by thinking of Georges Seurat's pointillist painting *Sunday Afternoon on the Island of La Grande Jatte*, an eight-foot panorama of people, parasols, water, and trees, all composed of tiny, identical-size dots of color. Consciousness would work the same way, according to Alexander, only on an invisible and universe-wide scope, our spirits merging after death in a vast expanse of energy. "In the realm of the super-small, every object in the physical universe is intimately connected with every other object. In fact, there are really no 'objects' in the world at all, only vibrations of energy, and relationships."[15]

But as I began to grasp the basis for Alexander's claims regarding how the brain, and the universe, functions, I also began to grasp why Sacks's claims had bothered me. He told the stories and drew conclusions, but his description of the science involved was cursory; his conclusions were not based on more than vague references to what went on in the brain. As always happens, as soon as I developed an awareness of the field of neurology, relevant articles began popping up. I soon realized that neither doctor stood on uncontested ground. A 2013 *New York Times* article about investigations by engineers into mind-controlled computers and smartphones implied that it would take ten years to map all of the brain, which of course meant that only a fraction of it was documented so far, and Sacks might be getting ahead of himself by ascribing visions of pink dwarfs to activity in one area of the cortex. Alison Gopnik, writing in the *Wall Street Journal*, thinks that trying to determine what part of the brain does what is mistaken, as, in her words, "most brain areas multitask," depending on an individual's focus of attention. But the real evidence that science did not yet have its ducks lined up, neurologically speaking, came with reviews of a recent revision of the mental health profession's handbook, the *Diagnostic and Statistical Manual of Mental Disorders*. Critical response revealed a striking amount of disagreement in the medical community, starting with the director of the National Institute of Mental Health, who challenged the book's scientific validity due to, as I understood it, a focus on symptoms rather than causes. Gary Greenberg, a practicing psychotherapist, called the new manual "a compendium of expert opinions masquerading as scientific truths."[16]

I had stumbled into a much larger debate, one between the scientific and the religious communities about the very nature of our life and our being. What is consciousness? What is the mind? What does it mean to "give up the ghost"? I realized that I had never taken my own research questions that seriously, thinking my quest relatively small and insignificant, not one with such grand implications. Reading Dr. Sacks and Dr. Alexander simultaneously, followed by a sampling of reviews and critiques, had forced me to examine what I could—and did—believe. While I would count on my common sense to cut through much of the scientific and philosophical material, these were questions I wasn't prepared to answer.

How did all of this change my own thoughts about what might, or might not, be going on in our house? Between hallucinations and sound vibrations, was there still room for a ghost?

I can recall three occasions on which I was so stunned by what I saw that I was momentarily paralyzed, speechless, unable to move or to articulate because what I saw was impossible. Once was when I was awakened in the middle of the night by crackling sounds. I got up and went to the window, where I saw, directly across the alley, a column of flames as tall and wide as our building. Another was when I opened the back door one morning and found my husband's new car sitting in its usual parking place but without wheels—neither tires, hubcaps, nor rims—the green Acura sedan balanced on its body like an insect carapace without legs.

My third experience occurred on the day I opened the secretary desk and found a hairbrush, the one that had disappeared six months earlier, stuffed into a cubbyhole.

There were explanations for the first two events. The column of flames was a major fire, one that had started in a brownstone opposite us that had been gutted for renovation; the fire had spread rapidly upward in the absence of internal barriers. The second was simple thievery. People well equipped for the job had removed all four wheels quickly and quietly and left the car sitting on two cement blocks and two plastic milk crates. I saw another car in a similar state two days later.

The third event, the discovery of the hairbrush, remains a mystery. I didn't hallucinate its presence in the cubbyhole, because it was really there! And sound vibrations didn't put that brush in the desk either. There had to be an explanation, for the brush and for other things that had happened: Dan's being pushed on the stairs by something invisible and Keith's laundry being folded when no one was home. These are mysteries for which the existence of a ghost might prove to be the only explanation.

CHAPTER NINE

MEDIUM AS MESSAGE

I may have been bereft of explanations, but what I did have was information, a lot of it, but all secondhand. I was up-to-date on the spirit world and the categories of professionals who make it their business to enable communication between the living and the no-longer living–clairvoyants, psychics, spiritualists, and the like–those people with special abilities who claim to see and converse with the dead. While I was on the fence about the validity of the results claimed by the ghost hunters–infrasound seemed to me to account for much of the activity picked up by detecting equipment–I was even less able to assess the claims of psychics and mediums. Certainly there were frauds, but there also seemed to be people who quite possibly weren't.

I'd begun thinking that I might have to get over my trepidation and visit a medium myself, actually interact with one of the people who are supposed to see and hear so much more than the rest of us, and then make an assessment based on my own face-to-face experience. I even began asking a few friends, people who had relayed ghost stories or told me they knew people who had seen ghosts, if they knew of anyone who had visited a medium and whether they would recommend him or her. I wasn't sure how to go about it; there were plenty of names of practitioners, many with testimonials, on the internet, but I really wanted a referral. And I wanted to know more about what was involved. Most of what I had read was taken from the medium's point of view (or from that of a debunker). What did one have to do, and what did it feel like, to be on the receiving end of the transaction?

A timely coincidence provided another, deeper level of information. I accompanied my husband to a business dinner that included a client visiting from California, a woman I'd met before and liked (her son and my daughter both live in New York, and we had tried to fix them up). When Don and several of his colleagues became embroiled in a discussion about Federal Reserve policy, Sandra turned and asked what I had been up to; we soon got into a conversation about ghosts. I told her that I was unsure about the notion that spirits of the dead can contact the living. A self-possessed and sophisticated woman of striking good looks, Sandra is not inclined to small talk or chatter. She leaned forward, looked me in the eye, and declared her own faith in spirits and in those who communicate with them. She also promised to send me a book that would explain a great deal about mediums and their abilities.

Having consumed one substantial martini and several glasses of wine, I remembered little of our discussion the next morning. But Sandra, having drunk sparingly, did remember, and upon her return home, she took the trouble to find and send me a hardcover copy of *The Eagle and the Rose*. I was pleased to see that the cover was a discreet blue with simple cream-colored block lettering; there was no Halloween-ish imagery, only a drawing of a gray-and-white feather.

Written by a British woman, Rosemary Altea, *The Eagle and the Rose* is the memoir of a "trance medium," a version of mediumship in which it is alleged that the spirit being contacted actually enters and temporarily takes control of the medium's mind and body. Altea explains that she discovered her psychic powers only when she was in her early thirties, having up until then believed that she was merely mad, as her grandmother had been. Suffering from nighttime visions all her life—as a child, the author saw vague faces and heard voices of a terrifying nature in the night—she was equally terrified of being thought mad and worked hard to control and camouflage her strange experiences, which continued into adulthood. Altea's home life was unhappy; she left school and married young, had a child, and eventually separated from her unfaithful husband. Years of penury and emotional distress followed, as she worked part-time in a rural pub to support herself and her child, leaving her house only to work. One evening a friend, concerned that Altea was becoming a recluse, insisted that she come out with her to a talk on tarot cards, playing cards used since the Middle Ages by psychics and fortune-tellers.

The talk was given at the home of a couple engaged in spiritualism. After the formal program, guests were asked to tell about their own paranormal experiences. When Altea claimed not to have had any, the host, a medium and healer, insisted that she speak. In a startling outburst, Altea told of her lifetime of peculiar experiences, including "the many times in my life I had been transported, as if by magic, to a different time or place in the universe." She then proceeded to go into a trance state, startling the other guests, in particular the friend who had brought her. But the host, assuring Altea that she wasn't crazy, told her later, "You are the greatest undeveloped medium my wife and I have ever met." He insisted she develop her powers. Initially resistant, Altea prayed for guidance and, when reassured that this path was God's will for her, began a course of instruction in becoming a medium.

I recalled the first "ghost" book I had read, medium Echo Bodine's *Relax, It's Only a Ghost*. Altea's story seemed to me to be very Bodine-like: the unexpected discovery of mediumistic ability, the initial reluctance, becoming convinced that one is doing God's will, development of psychic powers, embracing a new career, finding fame and fortune. But a significant chunk of Altea's story was different. While Bodine was mentored by a friendly local medium, Altea was told by her instructors that in time she would have her own special guide, someone from the spirit world who would help and lead her as she worked with spirits and those who wished to connect with them.

And this is where the book got silly. Finally, after she had committed herself to becoming a medium, taking instruction from other mediums and beginning to see clients, Altea's spirit guide made himself known to her, appearing one morning at her bedside in the guise of a Scotsman, wearing a kilt and all the rest of that nation's traditional regalia. Altea writes that she always liked Scottish people and was pleased with her guide; the two of them got along beautifully as she continued to work on her clairvoyant and clairaudient abilities, with his "helping, pushing, encouraging. . . . Every morning I would wake to find him smiling down at me and ready to begin another day. I was happy."[1] But the Scotsman was only a warm-up act. Several months later, during her weekly training session, Altea's true spirit guide appeared while she was in a trance state. "He was tall and broad, dark skinned, with shoulder-length black hair," she writes. "'My name,'" he said, "'is Grey Eagle, and I am Apache.'"[2]

Here my credulity not only stumbled but fell flat on its face. An American Indian? I grew up in Seattle, where Native

Americans were a vivid presence, their strong, literally chis-eled features staring out from the area's many totem poles. Schoolchildren are taught how the city is named for the wise and dignified Chief Sealth, who in the early 1800s chose not to attack the white-skinned newcomers but to work with them and in return secure the protection of tribal lands. I could not reconcile the idea of an Apache spirit guide with the image I had retained from childhood, the movie and television western por-trayal of the warlike Apaches, where the Native American male was a fierce warrior on a galloping horse. There was, I vaguely recalled, a tradition of Native peoples in the Southwest going off into the desert to achieve some sort of altered state, but this activity involved hallucinogens like peyote.

Even as I acknowledged being subject to gross stereotypes, I could not imagine a Native American male engaged in such a touchy-feely business. Apparently Rosemary Altea also found the idea of an Indian chief as spiritual guide difficult to accept. Reading up on what being a medium might entail, the author writes that, "The one thing that struck me more than anything else was that so many of these guides seemed to be American Indians. So farfetched did this seem to me at the time that I dis-missed it all as rubbish."[3]

How uninformed we both were! I, too, did some reading, and discovered that Native Americans are to shamanism as the French are to wine: the source, practitioners of a long and elaborate tradition, not the first, perhaps, but certainly the most developed. And for these shamans, birds are important mes-sengers from the spirit world; hence the feather on the book's cover.

Chief Grey Eagle becomes a major character in Altea's book. He accompanies the author on her rounds, appearing regularly by her bedside when she awakens and advising her as she grows into an "internationally renowned psychic and medium," according to the book jacket.

I Googled Rosemary Altea and found her prominence in the field to be well documented. She is so prominent, in fact, that the magicians Penn and Teller had taken it upon themselves to debunk her, much as Houdini had taken on the practices of prominent mediums a century earlier. Viewing tapes of a reading and consultation she had given, Penn and Teller pointed to the fact that she worked the room prior to the event, chatting with members of the audience and thereby gleaning personal information that she could later weave into her presentation.

Despite Penn and Teller, I persevered and read the remainder of *The Eagle and the Rose* carefully, knowing that I would have to write a detailed and thoughtful thank-you note to my friend Sandra. Much of the remainder of Altea's book was devoted to case studies, stories about people who needed to come to terms with tragedies involving the deaths of loved ones. The loved ones, when Altea and Grey Eagle could coax them to appear, often showed up for appointments early, such as the four-year-old girl who appeared while Altea was just getting out of bed. Clutching a teddy bear, the youngster told the author that her mother was coming for an appointment that day and she wanted Altea to be sure and tell her certain things; the little girl had been killed in an accident and her mother was hoping to communicate with her dead child. In fact, many of the spirits Altea summoned arrived dressed exactly as they had been in life and chatted up a storm of personal details, much as the spirits summoned by Echo Bodine were alleged to do. It was all very confusing, because even as I decided I could accept that there were spirit guides and that these spirit guides might well be Native Americans, I found it was the details, not the substance, that bothered me. Altea and Bodine went too far. The interactions with spirits seemed too elaborate, the dialogues too chatty in tone, the costumes and accessories too contrived. It was like telling a successful lie, I thought. Liars are advised to say as little as possible, just state the "facts" and not embroider. I wanted murky forms and disembodied voices, not golden-haired toddlers in smocked dresses clutching teddy bears.

Nonetheless, Altea's book was about as thorough a portrait of the medium's practice as any I was likely to find. Her description of going into the trance state, which would allow a spirit to enter her body, was riveting:

"I felt as if I were being drawn down into what I can only describe as a large black pit. . . . I seemed to be moving, floating, down, down, down. . . . As I traveled, in a kind of dreamlike state, farther and farther into this dark space, my limbs became heavy and my whole body became a dead weight. Then, in an instant and just in time, I realized what was happening. I was about to lose control of my conscious thoughts, to enter a trance state. My mind screamed out *No!* and I jerked myself back forcibly from the brink of unconsciousness."[4]

Altea explains that initially she was wary of the trance state because she did not want to lose control, but also because mediums often seemed to her to be faking trances, pretending that they had been taken over by a spirit. I knew what Oliver Sacks would have to say about this: that she was either hallucinating or self-hypnotized. But the point of the trance state, which Altea eventually would voluntarily enter, was to enable a spirit to enter and speak through the medium's body, and I find that any description of a medium's practice, whether genuine or suspicious, involves an initial mental focusing or concentrating. And I don't doubt that self-hypnotism is involved, blanking out the mind as it is said to do, casting out one's own thoughts so that a dead person's mind can move in.

The career training Altea describes, with its Apache Indian and dancing Scotsman, is so bizarre that I don't know what to make of it. And her writing style reminds me of a P. G. Wodehouse character, Madeleine Bassett, a young woman who seems always on the verge of baby talk. Fortunately, however, I could write Sandra and commend Altea's choice of an introductory quote from Pierre Teilhard de Chardin, a French philosopher and Jesuit priest, which opened up the whole giant question of who we really are and where we fit in the scheme of things: "We are not human beings having a spiritual experience. We are spiritual beings having a human experience."

I really needed to visit a medium myself, have the experience firsthand, and see how it affected my lingering skepticism. But I was still reluctant, partially because I couldn't think of what I would ask a medium—I had no recently deceased loved ones—but more because I was afraid. Of being duped? Of being manipulated? Of not being in control? I wasn't sure.

That Friday I left for our weekend house early. We'd had no rain all week, and I knew my flowers would be parched, so I was in a hurry to water them. A large rain barrel is positioned at the corner of the barn, handy to the two beds where I grow dahlias. As I stooped to pick up a watering can, I noticed a feather next to the barrel. It was a rather mangy feather, about eight inches long, but it had been stuck into the ground so that it stood straight up. Probably one of the boys who cut the grass put it there, I thought, but why? It was pale gray with a black tip, just like the one on the cover of Rosemary Altea's book.

※

CHAPTER TEN

I CONSULT A PSYCHIC, TIMIDLY

The feather was still in place when I went outside the next morning, the muted gray shaft holding its own among the leafy dahlia stalks. I bent over and picked it out of the ground. Just an ordinary feather, I thought as I examined it, the pattern and coloration unremarkable, a bit frayed at the tip, yet far too large to have been shed by one of the birds who frequent our yard: barn swallows, robins, goldfinches. While I resisted attaching significance to a random feather, it was too odd a coincidence; I had to accept it as some kind of sign. Were the Grey Eagles of the spirit world sending a "you need to take us more seriously" message?

Clearly I needed to get over my reluctance and schedule a session with a psychic. I suddenly recalled that two years earlier, while visiting a favorite shop near my daughter's West Village apartment, I had picked up a flyer about a psychic, Anne Cervone, who would be giving readings during a book-signing event. The shop's owner was from Boston, and we had fallen into conversation; she told me that this particular psychic had been extraordinarily prescient with regard to her brother, who had turned out to have a terminal illness. Did I still have the flyer? Yes, miraculously, and I determined to call her. It was just like what I used to do when I was writing cases, I told myself: call people, make an appointment, and conduct an interview. But what would I say? I couldn't feign interest in contacting the spirit world, despite the fact that most of my family now resides there. Insofar as the future was concerned, I didn't want to know anything about my own; I preferred to live my life as it unfolded, and at my age there were few major developments likely in the areas of career and romance. The only thing I did want to know was if and when my thirty-five-year-old daughter was going to marry; Elizabeth doesn't confide details of her social life, and I've had no choice but to wait and see. But I just couldn't countenance such an invasion of her privacy.

I dialed Ms. Cervone and got an answering machine, so I left my number. The next morning I tried again. She did not return my call, and I could not locate her on the internet. I concluded that she had moved or retired, or, possibly, that her contacts in the spirit world had told her I was a skeptic and should be avoided. But while I was relieved that my psychic experience had been postponed, I had taken the first step and was determined to continue. I wanted to find a psychic or medium who came recommended, not some random name from the yellow pages or the internet, so I began asking around, checking with people I thought might know of someone. It turned out to be like asking about plastic surgery: approached discreetly, almost everyone admits to having had some procedure. "I don't know why consulting psychics isn't more mainstream," one woman commented. "Everybody does it."

A young woman I knew through a speaker series at our

church, "Art and Spirituality," gave me the email address of a male parishioner, Stephen, who had consulted a psychic and found him helpful; she also told me about another church member, Marie, who had engaged a psychic to deal with negative energy in one part of her house. I knew both of these people, vaguely, and that evening I emailed Stephen, explaining what I was doing and wondering if he could recommend someone in the psychic world. I received the following reply:

"Happy to tell you what I learned. I did have some sessions many years ago with a 'channeler.' . . . I'm not sure if this is considered a form of medium, but my sense is when we move into this dimension, it doesn't really matter so much what we call it, rather it is about their ability to tune into the various levels of consciousness where spirits who are currently not incarnate dwell.

"Kirk, the channeler, would go into a trance, and a spirit named Charles would 'come through' and speak directly to me. We spent a lot of time talking about my past lives and their influence on my current life. . . . For instance, in my most recent previous life, I came under the care of the Church of England as a young choir boy, and later went into the priesthood. I died in 1941 in Bristol, England, as a parish priest. All of this is so elegantly simple in explaining my love of English choral music."

I read the email twice, stupefied, both by the content and by the person who had sent it, as I knew that Stephen was active in the church and worked for one of Boston's most venerable law firms. That a lawyer and devout Episcopalian not only consorted with "channelers" but also believed them was a revelation. Stephen added that he had lost touch with Kirk, thought he had moved, but would try to track him down if need be. I declined, thinking that Kirk's area of expertise was quite different, having to do with reincarnation, and were I to use him, I'd have to get

my mind around a whole new aspect of spiritualism, to say nothing of possibly confronting my former selves.

Another friend told me about her neighbor Pat, who had
seen a medium after the suicide of a young man who had lived
with her family for several years. She thought that Pat had found
the sessions extremely helpful. I emailed Pat and received a
name—Kevin—and the number for a psychic practice called Circle of Believing. Pat explained, "Kevin works in a specific way,
needing a picture of the person he is connecting with. I find him
emotionally distant but stunningly accurate." She added that she
had on another occasion met with Lorraine, the owner of the
practice, and found her helpful also.

I decided I would try Kevin or Lorraine, but Circle of Believing turned out to be located in a town north of Boston where
I'd never been. If I were going to confront the spirit world in
person, I thought I would prefer to do it in a familiar neighborhood. I followed up on several other leads, but they proved to
be dead ends: one contact had lost an unlisted number, another
said the psychic she consulted had moved to the West Coast. I
spoke with Marie, the woman who was supposed to have hired
a psychic to deal with negative energy in her house, and was told
she had engaged a feng shui practitioner who had rearranged the
furniture.

Circle of Believing seemed to be my best bet, so I called
and asked for an appointment. It was then mid-October, and the
woman who answered told me that Kevin was no longer with
the practice, and Lorraine was booking appointments for February. "Oh no," I protested, "that's way too far off!" She offered to
put me on the cancellation list.

Once again I'd put off my face-to-face with a psychic, but
with all the inquiries I'd been making, I was likely to be seeing
someone soon, and, deep down, I was less than thrilled at the

prospect. How would I behave? I really didn't want to make contact with any dead person. I wanted to know how the whole thing worked, how an individual with alleged special powers managed to summon the spirit of a deceased human being. I wanted to see and hear with my own eyes and ears. But how could I avoid being fooled, seduced by a skilled con artist into believing whatever he or she might tell me, leaving the session convinced that there was an accessible spirit world, when in fact I'd just been hoodwinked? Bernie Madoff, jailed some years ago after perpetrating the biggest swindle of all time, remained a vivid memory; we knew one older couple, both savvy business-people, who had lost everything and been forced to sell their house and art collection. Madoff's ability to fabricate financial statements credible to sophisticated investors was proof that all of us are inclined to believe what we want to. For a clever psychic with decent perceptual abilities and access to the internet, figuring out what Jeanne Stanton might like to hear would be a piece of cake.

But it really wasn't that I was afraid of being fooled. I was afraid of *not* being fooled. What made me squeamish, I'd begun to realize, was being in such an unfamiliar situation, one whose structure and outcome I couldn't anticipate, or worse, control. Might I have my past and possibly my future laid out before me, my hopes and dreams, my fears and delusions, revealed by a stranger who could literally see through me? This was a fright-ening prospect. As was the prospect of confronting my mother, who, I felt sure, would even as a spirit have retained her ability to push my buttons. And does anyone really want to talk to their dead relatives? I loved both of my grandmothers, but I couldn't imagine conversing with them after more than thirty years. Beyond "I miss you" and "I still love you," what could I tell them that they, as spirits, wouldn't already know?

I decided to call Pat and ask if she would describe her experience to me in detail, and in that way I could at least have a sense of what it was like. She agreed and we met for lunch a week later.

Pat Hunt is a woman I've seen around the neighborhood for years; we are about the same age and have many mutual friends. It turned out to be one of those six-degrees-of-separation things, as Jack, the young man whose suicide had prompted her to consult a medium, was someone I'd met. He had been a high school pal of one of our babysitters, and I remembered him because he was so personable, a teenager whose conversational skills belied his years. Pat gave me the following background: Jack, who had developed a successful career as a builder, had done a renovation project for Pat's family, and later lived for a time in a small apartment in their town house. He was like a member of the family and was particularly close to her teenage children. Then Jack fell on hard times. His business failed, and a lover abandoned him. He moved back in with Pat's family and became involved with a new person. But things were worse than they appeared. One Saturday Jack told Pat that he was going to a local beach for a swim. He never came back.

When Jack's body was recovered days later, the family learned that he had become addicted to heroin and as a result was bankrupt financially, emotionally, and physically. The shock of his death, followed by these revelations, was particularly hard on Pat's daughter, who regarded Jack as a brother. Someone suggested that trying to make contact with his spirit might console her. That was how Pat found her way to Kevin and Circle of Believing.

She made an appointment for herself first. "I went in not at all nervous," Pat told me. "I thought it would be bullshit. But I wanted to find out if there was anything in it that would help my daughter to feel better." I asked her to tell me as much as she could remember about the session. "Kevin is a flight attendant who does this in his spare time, mainly for extra money," she said. "He had asked me to bring a picture and I did, a headshot of Jack without any revealing details. 'Jack's gay' was the first thing he said when he looked at the picture. Then, 'I'm hearing suicide.' He went on to tell me other things about Jack and our family that were totally accurate.

"He also told me to write things down as he talked," Pat added, "asking, 'Does that make sense?' and telling me that it might make sense later. He said he saw some seashells that had moved recently. And he reassured me, saying that Jack would be with us occasionally in Vermont, where we have a second home."

We then talked about my project and Pat said that, for my purposes, meeting with Lorraine, the woman who ran Circle of Believing, would be more useful. While Lorraine did not have Kevin's mediumistic powers and was less able to home in on targeted spirits, she was more holistic in her psychic practice. I wasn't sure what *holistic* meant in this context, but I did know that homing in on a targeted spirit was something I hoped to avoid.

Later I reviewed my notes and realized I didn't really understand the part about the shells, so I emailed Pat and asked her to elaborate. She replied as follows:

"Jack died at Crane Beach. About three or four days after his death, I went there and just spent some time. I picked up some shells and one smooth stone and decided to keep them in his memory. When I came home, I placed them on a shelf where they remained for about nine months. One day I decided to throw out several of them, but I kept the stone and two shells. I moved them to a cabinet in my bedroom. Shortly after this, I went to see Kevin and one of the things he told me was, 'I'm hearing that some shells were moved recently.'"

This remarkable piece of the account was for me the bit that gave credence to everything else. Such a particular and private bit of information! And after hearing Pat's description of the process, I realized that mediums were not judgmental, nor even that perceptive—they simply reported what was being told to them, much as a telephone transmits a voice. Hence the detachment Pat credited to Kevin. He was only a conduit.

Now I actually wanted to see a psychic. The flyer from the woman in New York was still on my desk—should I track her down? As it turned out, I didn't have to. On the following day I returned home to find Circle of Believing on my caller ID. I called the number and was told that Lorraine had decided to open up her vacation week, and I could see her at three o'clock on October 31, Halloween.

I had a week to prepare, and I began drafting questions. Essentially I wanted to know about *her*, not about me, so I tried to formulate questions like, "How did you learn about your powers?" and "Why do only some people have these abilities?" I also felt I should be prepared to claim interest in contacting someone from the spirit world, but as I mentally scanned my list of deceased relatives and friends for someone I'd really like to talk to, I was at a loss. Later, as I was undressing for bed, I spied a small picture of my uncle Ken among the photos and clippings on a bulletin board that hangs next to my closet. It had been there for nearly ten years, hidden under a changing gallery of photos and pages torn from fashion magazines. Ken had died in his sleep while living at my grandmother's house in Seattle; when I learned of his death, I'd rooted around in a box of old photos and found a snapshot he had sent me in 1982. He was standing on the deck of a ship, choppy water in the background, smiling in that goofy, childlike way he had. His graying hair was thick and wavy and uncharacteristically long.

Ken was my father's older half brother, a bachelor who had been part of our family life for as long as I could remember. While he worked on merchant ships and so was away at sea much of the time, when Ken was home he was often at our house, occasionally babysitting my sister and brother and me, which we loved, because he would give us ice cream at the start of dinner, and once, when our parents were away overnight, he let us have ice cream for breakfast. Uncle Ken was always making jokes, often at his own expense. But he had a contrary streak, too, and a favorite family story was based on the time he brought my grandmother, who lived in downtown Seattle, on a rare visit to our rural home on Bainbridge Island. My grandmother didn't drive, never had, but she had supplied a spirited critique of Ken's driving during the five-mile trip from the ferry terminal. She was still at it when they walked in the door.

Well, Uncle Ken had the last word. When they left, we saw him back his car up the driveway, and we later learned that he had continued backing it for the entire five miles, turning around only when they reached the outskirts of Winslow.

I could imagine slipping easily into conversation with Uncle Ken. I'd ask him what it was like being dead and undoubtedly he would have a funny story about his life on the other side.

On the day of my appointment, I tucked a sheet of questions into my notebook and, after studying it, my photo of Uncle Ken. I got driving instructions for 270 Main Street from MapQuest. It looked like a pretty simple trip, and in fact it was: straight up I-93 for about fifteen miles to Exit 40, turn right, then left, then another left, and I was there. Main Street proved to be a bland, commercial strip; Circle of Believing was across from a copy center and a Stop and Shop and next door to a Dairy Queen, in the kind of modest office complex that, in small towns, typically houses professional offices. Sure enough, the directory for the two-story colonial-style building listed a law firm, an accountant, an insurance broker, and a financial planner, as well as a beauty salon and a cosmetic laser clinic. Circle of Believing was on the second floor, and so I climbed the stairs, opened the door, and found myself in a dimly lit and copiously furnished room that had a large television mounted in one corner. There were several large, deep sofas and chairs, draped with shawls and filled with pillows. Four small bedside table lamps provided the only light. It was like the female version of a man cave.

A young woman clad in jeans and a Gap hoodie sat behind a small desk in one corner; she had just unpacked her lunch, and the smell of chili wafted from a Styrofoam container. "Lorraine is running late," she told me. "I tried to call you. We had to move your appointment to three forty-five." This gave me ample time to examine the rest of the furnishings, which included a series of framed Pre-Raphaelite prints featuring King Arthur, Guinevere, and Ophelia; bookshelves holding volumes that ranged from the Kama Sutra to astrology to Deepak Chopra; a glass case holding a selection of candles, oils, and incense powder, all with price tags; several artificial plants; family photos; and a framed document stating that Lorraine was a certified notary public.

The office was also decorated for Halloween, with spiders, cobwebs, and a small skeleton dangling in one corner.

Unless one wanted to read, the room was comfortable and no doubt reassuring to clients who might be nervous or bereft; they could lounge, nap, or watch TV, which during my wait featured some kind of game show. Finally the office door opened, and a woman emerged. Laughing, she turned to continue whatever conversation she and Lorraine were having, pausing in the doorway for several minutes. Then it was my turn. An attractive middle-aged woman with streaked brown hair, Lorraine was seated behind a large cluttered desk. I sat in a chair opposite her.

It was clear why Lorraine had run late—she talked a blue streak. Once I explained how I'd gotten there—the happenings in my house, my exploration of the paranormal, hearing about Pat's experience with Kevin, and becoming more and more inclined to credit the existence of spirits—she broke in. "I am recently a widow," she began. "My husband died four months ago, unexpectedly." She explained that her husband had a medical condition and was careless about adhering to the doctor's orders, and she was really angry about his dying. "But," she continued, "now he talks to me every night. He talks—through thought—and I write. I write pages and pages in this book." She held up an open notebook whose lined pages were packed with longhand.

I'd begun taking notes, explaining that I was writing a book about my house, but I couldn't keep up. Either I was talking or Lorraine was, she so fast that I had to pay careful attention. It was like the economics class I took in graduate school; the professor tore through material that was totally new to me, and I soon realized that I could either try to take notes or try to understand what she was saying.

Lorraine began to talk about the spirits in my house, saying that she saw a woman holding a child, as well as a man. "Death," she said suddenly. "I sense a death, a child. It could have been an accident. I feel choking, suffocation." I said I didn't know; it was possible. Lorraine also said that there was a portal in our house, and spirits were coming in who hadn't necessarily lived there. I should be careful not to attract more of them by using something like a Ouija board. I found myself picturing a porthole, as in a ship, through which wispy forms were whooshing in and out. But before I could develop this image further, Lorraine was on to something else. She had spread out a deck of cards, facedown. I was to select ten. I picked out the cards, which had a small blue pattern on the back, one by one, not turning them over, and handed them to her. She arranged them in three vertical rows, face up, commenting, "Let's see what's going on here."

"Are boats important in your family?" Lorraine asked. "I see boats, big boats." I explained that both my father and my uncle had worked on ships (she had not seen my picture of Uncle Ken). She began to talk about my father, saying that she saw a very imposing man, broad-shouldered and very handsome. All true. We continued. Lorraine surmised several things that were spot-on, such as that I didn't get along with my sister (we had different kinds of energy, she said), and several that weren't, such as that someone was giving my husband a hard time at the office (no one, so far as I knew). Insofar as the spirits in my house were concerned, she advised me to take a lot of pictures in areas where we had experienced activity, and said that eventually I would see orbs of light in the photos where the spirits were. I should also try to communicate by writing. "They like that you are writing about them," Lorraine assured me. If I talked to them and said I wanted to communicate, a response would come via the pen I held. Further, it would be hard for us to sell the house because the spirits wouldn't want us to leave. They would create a negative energy that would deter buyers.

My time was up, but Lorraine kept on, saying she was interested in what was going on in my house and would visit me, free of charge. That was a surprise, and it was probably an offer I shouldn't refuse. Trying to sort out my feelings as I walked to my car, I found that I liked Lorraine; my instinct for something being off hadn't kicked in, and she just seemed genuinely interested in what I had to tell her. Lorraine had taken charge of the session but not in a way that was offensive or intimidating, and while much of what she said was inaccurate—I'd say 40 percent— it could have been her misinterpretation of whatever information she was receiving. Before our meeting, I'd rather hoped to be able to cross off the Lorraines of the world, but it really did seem that she had the capacity to explain a great many things. Which, of course, was what I was supposed to think: that was why Pat had gone back several times and why Lorraine's schedule was booked months in advance. But, I reminded myself, my goal was to find out if we had a ghost, and if so, who it was. Lorraine was the first person I'd met who might have some answers.

❊

CHAPTER ELEVEN

SHERLOCK HOLMES AND THE LURE OF BELIEVING

W hen you travel with children, an older friend once told me, it's an entirely different experience. You see the world through their eyes. Since I had been traveling in the paranormal world, I had begun to feel that I was seeing through many sets of eyes: those of mediums like Echo Bodine and Lorraine, of medical authorities such as neurologist Oliver Sacks, of the hosts of *Ghost Adventures*, of all the friends like my neighbor Cheryl who had shared their own ghost stories, as well as the others who were incredulous that I would embark on such a project. Now I was on my way to confer with Lorraine again, hoping for her help in narrowing the field of ghost candidates; I had brought a tape recorder so I could look and listen without the distraction of note-taking.

My appointment was at noon, but when I arrived, there was no Lorraine, only her assistant, Nancy, busy returning calls and scheduling appointments. It was a sunny day, and I could see the room more clearly; while much was the same, the Hallow-een decorations were gone and only a single green Easter egg suspended on a ribbon marked the season. The artificial plants had proliferated, however, with large clumps of plastic wisteria dangling from the ceiling and draped over the window frames.

Lorraine finally arrived at 12:40. Her dark blond hair was shorter, styled in a smooth chin-length bob, and she wore a tai-lored print dress and low heels; except for the dangling hoop earrings, her outfit was similar to what I remember my mother wearing as proprietor of a small-town real estate firm, what I'd call "suburban business." We began somewhat haltingly, as I had to remind Lorraine why I was there, but she soon perked up and we were off. Lorraine began to describe her sense of a child, death, and multiple spirits passing through my house. I spoke of my attempts at automatic writing, and Lorraine was adamant that it would work. I needed to be patient and to start off the process by just writing, describing my day perhaps, "journal-ing." Eventually spirits would join in. She also explained, when I reported having no sense anymore of a presence in the house, that the spirits would return with the warmer weather. This seemed absurd to me. Why should ghosts care about weather? But then I remembered that Bodine had described spirits as having low energy, and how they often needed to inhabit a live person, absorbing their energy in order to function during visits on this side. Just like a car battery, I thought, sluggish if left too long in the cold.

At the end of the hour, Lorraine offered once again to visit my house and take a look herself. This time, however, she wanted to bring a friend, one of her professional colleagues. And she wanted us to be alone with no distractions. My husband should not be at home. This was getting too weird, I thought. I hadn't learned much that was new this time, and her stipulations seemed odd. I took down her cell number and said I would call, knowing that I most likely wouldn't.

What I didn't tell Lorraine during our session was that my automatic writing attempts had been brief and desultory: I would take a pad and pen to Laura's room, then to my room, sit for three or four minutes in each location, and then get fidgety. The three times I had tried automatic writing, my impatience—and inability to sit still—had truncated what should have been a more open-ended, thoughtful process. I would try again and try harder.

At ten thirty on a May morning, I gathered my writing materials, climbed the stairs to Laura's room, settled myself on the chaise in front of her bookcase, and began writing:

"I am sitting in Laura's room, since it has been a site for spirit activity. It is the former nursery and used to have a connecting door to the little room next to it. Could whoever might have been visiting be the spirit of a child? The maiden aunt? Or, as I've always suspected, could it be one of the old doctors, dropping in to suggest Laura's career path? She spent so much time lying awake in this room, thanks to her chronic insomnia. Did she ever see anything? And if she did, would she tell me?

"It's a bright, almost sunny morning, maybe not the best time for spirits." At this point I happened to look up, saw myself reflected in the floor-length mirror opposite, sitting on the chaise, rows of books behind me. I thought I looked normal enough. "There's her high school graduation picture on top of the bookcase, all those girls kneeling in their white dresses. And next to it is Michael Mazur's etching of a scene from *The Inferno* that we gave her for college graduation. She wanted it because she wrote her thesis on Dante. I keep forgetting that Laura minored in Italian, which isn't surprising, since she hasn't uttered a word about Italy since her semester in Venice.

"Across from me is the window where I used to stand and look down into the nursery school classroom, easy to see into because it is in the ground floor of the church across the street. Seated here I can see into the top-floor windows of the town house next to it. There are candlestick lamps with white shades and one of those pyramid-tower sculptures that decorators like. Stacks of books. I am tempted to get the binoculars.

"So much history in this room! There's the chest of drawers we had painted specially for Laura, a creamy base with peach and pale blue trim, and on the bottom drawer a life-size rendering of our dear departed cat Pamplemousse. And underneath the chest I can see the edge of a box wrapped in white paper. Laura's wedding dress is inside, cleaned and carefully folded, the stains on the hem removed with great difficulty, according to the woman from Jean Palmer Cleaners. On the bedside table there's a photo of Laura and her friend Lara lounging on the Winsor playing field. Are they watching a game? Studying outside? I can't tell; it's just an idyllic scene I've always loved. The floral print draperies—roses, lilies of the valley—are from the shop where Laura worked during school vacations.

"The books behind me are mostly school texts, high school's *Mill on the Floss* and the *Poems of Catullus* yielding shelf space to college's *Fundamentals of Behavioral Statistics* and *Theories of Personality*. The stereo is gone because I removed it several months ago in a decluttering effort. The mantel holds a half-dozen framed photos, graduation pictures, Laura with her best friend from high school, Susannah, another with her best friend from college, Barbara. There is a snapshot of Laura giving our Scottish terrier Macduff a bath, the same dog who, I now recall, as a puppy chewed a hole in this carpet, then brand-new. I was so mad I yelled at Laura and the dog until I was hoarse. Her old bed is gone, the curvy cast-iron one replaced by a queen-size bed with a plain linen headboard, less fanciful but far better suited to her husband's six-foot-five frame."

I glanced at my watch. Thirty-five minutes had passed and all the writing was mine. Should I sit in Liz's room for a while? Or should I try my own bedroom, scene of the disappearing hairbrush?

I went downstairs and sat in the tufted Victorian chair, which wore its own history in the faded green velvet upholstery, with spots here and there, the arms worn and dingy after years of Don's pushing himself back up to a standing position after sitting down to tie his shoes.

"This room is greatly changed," I write. "We have a different bed, new artwork has been added over the years, and the photos on the mantel now range from our children as toddlers to one of Laura in her wedding dress, posing with her bouquet on the lawn in front of Trinity Church, several groomsmen and that grotesque white limo she wanted visible in the background. The walls are now a color I'd call cantaloupe, formerly a rather gloomy blue-green."

After twenty minutes or so I stopped writing. I felt nothing in this room and, as I had told Lorraine, hadn't for a long time. Perhaps the ghost who hid the brush didn't like the new color scheme. But I wondered if it wasn't the lack of children, because since I had been sitting for an hour and considering these bedrooms, I realized that was the biggest change of all. The girls had been gone from their own rooms for years, but they were gone from our bedroom, too. They were always in this room, first thing in the morning and last thing at night, getting dressed, watching TV, just hanging out. But for the past dozen years it had been just Don and me.

Why was I even thinking like this? It was one thing to suspend disbelief, to give ghosts a chance, but my disbelief had been suspended for quite a while. I, who at the suggestion of a psychic, had been sitting in various rooms of my house with pad and pencil, waiting for something to happen, suddenly realized it was time to take stock. Where was I in my search? What had I learned? Was any of it relevant, or was I going too far afield?

A few nights earlier I had been watching the latest *Sherlock* episodes on the *Masterpiece Mystery* series. Besides being entranced by Benedict Cumberbatch, the most recent, and to my eyes, the most appealing Sherlock ever, I was a lifelong Sherlock Holmes fan. What came to mind just now was how different this durable hero was from his creator. I wondered at how the Holmes character, a paragon of logic and rationality, could be conjured up by an author who was, by the end of his life, the antithesis. I knew from my reading that, in his later years, Arthur Conan Doyle was besotted with the new religion of Spiritualism and the alleged power of mediums to contact the deceased. An enormous discrepancy developed between the fiction Doyle wrote and the fiction he eventually lived. How had this happened, and was I headed in the same direction?

Somewhere I had two big books on Doyle, with all of his Holmes stories and accompanying biographical data. I put down my writing materials and went to the shelves on the landing outside our bedroom, where I keep all of "my" books—my college texts, all the novels I've read in the last thirty years, biographies, gardening books, travel diaries. I found the Holmes books right away, two oversized volumes that constitute William S. Baring-Gould's *Annotated Sherlock Holmes*.[1] Arthur Conan Doyle, I read, the son of an aristocratic but impoverished and broken Edinburgh family, began writing the Holmes stories just after he had married, started his own medical practice, and found himself with bills to pay. He modeled his hero on a former university professor renowned for his powers of observation and deduction, Dr. Joseph Bell, who later wrote to his former student, "You are yourself Sherlock Holmes and well you know it." The Holmes stories seem consistent with a nonreligious medical man's point of view, as the detective inevitably finds that very real human mendacity is at the root of all the evil he encounters. In "Hound of the Baskervilles," published in 1901 and one of his best-known stories, Doyle uses the Gothic tradition to introduce supernatural elements—an ancient curse, a mysterious beast—to set the stage. Sherlock Holmes, always attracted by bizarre occurrences, uses observation and logic to dismantle the murderous scheme of a disaffected family member.

Doyle's reasons for making Sherlock Holmes aloof, prickly, and a cocaine addict are not clear to me, as nothing in his biography suggests that Hall or Doyle was atypically arrogant, devoid of emotion, or a user of drugs. But Conan Doyle did, as Hall observed, mirror the methods and accomplishments of his hero, assisting the police on important cases; Doyle was a lifelong seeker of justice and conducted two famous investigations that freed men previously convicted of serious crimes. But while Sherlock with his scientific approach seems to be who Dr. Arthur Conan Doyle was for much of his life, an emotionally and intellectually unkempt spiritualist was who Doyle became.

Baring-Gould was not informative about Conan Doyle's spiritualist beliefs and practices. I went to Wikipedia to learn that Doyle suffered greatly after the death of his first wife in 1906. In fact, it was after a number of family deaths—beginning with his wife and followed by the deaths of a son, a brother, two brothers-in-law, and two nephews during and just after the First World War—that Doyle sank into a severe depression. Spiritualism, with its premise that those we love are accessible beyond the grave, brought such comfort that Doyle became an ardent proselytizer. He wrote extensively on spiritualism during the 1920s and defended prominent mediums when they were accused of trickery, even some of the more blatant and well-documented crooks. Unable to deal with any contradictory data, Doyle even argued with the famous magician Harry Houdini, who, himself seeking solace after his mother's death, attended dozens of séances, where he found only other magicians and the usual tricks. "It's all an illusion," Houdini supposedly told Doyle, "just like what I do. I've no special powers, only clever tricks that fool the eye." "No," Doyle apparently protested. "You are wrong. You do have supernatural powers."

Sir Arthur Conan Doyle had become, I concluded, a shining example of how far afield believing what we want to can take us. The Wikipedia entry referred to a public debate between Doyle and Joseph McCabe, the latter an ordained Catholic priest who had left the church to become a writer and speaker with a distinctly atheistic point of view. After the debate, in which he challenged an intransigent Doyle to defend numerous proofs of duplicity connected to spiritualism, McCabe expanded his arguments into a book, *Is Spiritualism Based on Fraud?* Curious about the nature of McCabe's position, I was delighted to be able to access online the entire 1920 publication, turning the pages of the small, cloth-covered volume on my computer screen. "Mediums are the priests of the spiritualist religion," McCabe begins. "They are the indispensable channels of communication with the other world. They have, not by anointing, but by birthright, the magical character which fits them alone to perform the miracle of the new revelation. . . . Were they to form a union or go on strike, the life of the new religion would be more completely suspended than the life of any other religion."[2]

This was certainly true insofar as my own experience was concerned. I could hardly argue with Lorraine about what she herself claimed to perceive. Much of her commentary had been accurate.

There weren't any real facts or figures I could argue with, or enough countervailing data to discredit what she had told me.

McCabe was as thorough as Sherlock Holmes would have been in his deconstruction of alleged mediumistic powers, explaining how low light, dark drapery, and phosphorous were used at séances to create the illusion of visiting spirits. Further, he pointed out that the voluminous nature of Victorian female clothing allowed considerable secreting of objects and sound sources. And he echoed my own concern with the as-in-life appearance of the spirits summoned by the contemporary mediums I'd studied, Echo Bodine and Rosemary Altea: they "saw" so much in the way spirits were dressed, despite our supposedly leaving our substantive selves, including outfits and jewelry, behind us at death! "Was the next world," McCabe writes, "a material world, full of color, clothes, and flowers?"

Writing almost a century ago, McCabe ticked off every single tool in the medium's kit—clairvoyance, telepathy, automatic writing (!)—as he meticulously described each and every documented spiritualist phenomenon and cited definitive proof that all reported supernatural events had been fabricated. In one particularly colorful example featuring spirit messages, he describes the methods of two Chicago mediums, the Misses Bangs, who provided letters from deceased relatives during sittings via a method involving dim lights and pulling trays with stationery by a string running under a covered table. As crude as it was, this deception worked until a suspicious client submitted the name of a relative who obligingly wrote back, despite never having existed.

Already I had accepted that the sense I sometimes had of a "presence," as well as the sound of doors slamming and footsteps on the stairs, could possibly be attributed to vibrations or temperature changes. Perhaps I had dreamed the shadow on the stairs, and Laura only thought she saw Rita in the laundry room, when it had been something like a dress or a skirt and blouse hung up to dry. Maybe the cleaning woman somehow moved Elizabeth's very heavy bed before we left and we just hadn't noticed. But did the cat play the piano? I am positive she didn't, and both Don and I heard it. What happened to Dan on the stairs? Who folded Keith's laundry? These remained events without plausible explanations, as did that very singular first incident, the placement of the hairbrush in the secretary desk.

But McCabe was entirely correct. To get any further along the road to certainty, I would have to rely on those who had a monopoly on the pipeline, those alleged to know, the critical word being *alleged*. The information I might obtain with respect to the presence and identity of ghosts in my house would be only as valid as the source of that information. What if genuine psychics and mediums—unlike McCabe, I believe there are honest practitioners—are capable of transmitting misinformation, due to their own credulity or to a misinterpretation of whatever information they are given?

It occurred to me, as I thought about how Lorraine described the way in which she wrote out her husband's thoughts each night, that whatever she produced on paper could simply be the product of her own subconscious desire. Why couldn't Lorraine, whose husband had been dead only four months, have been writing out the kinds of things she wanted to hear from him, the kinds of things she *had* heard from him, during the long years of their marriage? While psychics—much like surrealist artists—claim supernatural control of their writing arm, psychologists posit a close connection between the hand that writes and the brain that provides both mechanical function and its content.

I also recalled an article by Malcolm Gladwell I'd read some years ago about the special talent of certain people to foresee outcomes.[3] The examples cited were a surgeon and an athlete, extraordinarily successful in their respective fields. The author described how each seemed able to do what they did so well because they were able to know the outcome before they acted; that is, if the scalpel moved a certain way, or the ball arched at a certain angle, specific results would follow, despite volatile, uncertain conditions. Most likely, both had not clairvoyance but something very like it, the kind of genius that allows the brain to process relevant information so quickly and adroitly that the likely results are known and the optimum action selected with what seems like superhuman speed. Much of what passed for psychic power, perhaps, was simply a much better than average ability, based on both talent and years of practice, to predict outcomes.

And perhaps I, who did not claim any but the most average perceptive ability, could accomplish a bit more on my own. But I had been prevented—had prevented myself—from taking the initiative because of the hospitable attitude I had adopted toward the ghost. One thing I'd been advised to do, and had resisted doing, was to try to take a picture of the ghost. I'd actually had the idea myself early on, thinking that if I had set up a camera on a tripod next to the piano, with very slow exposure, I might eventually get an image of whatever was moving across the room as I practiced. An immediate problem would be the amount of visual interference, with reflections off the windows and cars going by; I'd done enough photography to know how easily undetected foreign elements can incorporate themselves into an image. But what really prevented me was a reluctance I felt to do something that somehow seemed rude. I had already, apparently, attributed certain characteristics to our anonymous ghost, among these a Boston Brahmin decorum. If it were old Dr. Putnam or any of his family members, I felt such surreptitious attempts to obtain an image would be highly inappropriate.

Nor, for that matter, would they knowingly parade back and forth in front of my camera.

Clearly I had not only accepted, but forged a kind of bond with our ghost, encompassing a code of behavior I attributed to our invisible but most likely Victorian-era guest. This posture of mine, I was beginning to understand, could be dangerous. "Don't make a pet of a ghost!" Echo Bodine warned in her book. She was concerned about keeping a distressed and possibly destructive spirit from commuting to the other side. I was concerned about my attachment to our ghost, that it was making me too credulous, too eager to accept information that seemed to verify its existence. And my attitude about the whole ghost project, the research I had undertaken, had shifted significantly over the months and years.

In the beginning I was self-conscious about my quest, even embarrassed by it, and so relieved that I could sit at my computer or in the Boston Public Library and read up on the world of spirits without anyone knowing what I was doing. It was like reading porn. I kept my materials hidden from view when I worked in the library, not wanting the young man with the laptop across the table from me to see that I was reading a book with what looked like Casper the Friendly Ghost on the cover. I didn't tell people what I was trying to write about, except in a joking way, as in, "Oh, people seem interested, so I am doing some research on the ghost, giggle, giggle." But as my family became more accepting, and friends began showing a genuine interest in my subject matter, I became emboldened, talking freely about the various things that had happened in our house. This led to further reinforcement of my project, as even new acquaintances eagerly told me their own stories. Just last week, the young man who manages an art gallery we frequent told me about the ghosts he has had to pacify in his new vacation home, an eighteenth-century colonial. "I just stood in the center of the house and said, 'Okay, we are glad you are here, and we hope to live peacefully with you in your house.'"

I'd also been forced to admit that I liked having the ghost in the house. When a friend had suggested that I engage an exorcist, I'd resisted, protesting that our ghost was not frightening or destructive. I didn't want it to go away, and I actually worried during the long period when it seemed to have gone, wondering if we had done something to offend it. The ghost had become like an imaginary friend to whom I had assigned a vague identity. It was only as real as I chose to make it.

The business of psychics had opened a Pandora's box. I had suspended disbelief sufficiently to not only visit a psychic but to prepare beforehand for a possible conversation with a dead relative. And I had been favorably impressed with Lorraine's abilities. Was I going the same way as Arthur Conan Doyle?

Then I remembered Pat's seashells, and Kevin, the part-time psychic who knew about them because he had received some form of message from the dead man, Jack. *Yes,* I reminded myself, *there is more here than meets the eye.*

I've always been fascinated by Henry James's novella, *The Turn of the Screw.* It isn't the story so much as how it came to be written that appeals to me (although the story of two children possessed by demons is eerie enough). It was conceived during the time when many scholars and scientists, including Henry's brother William, were actively involved in investigations of the spirit world through entities like the Ghost Club and the Society for Psychical Research. While there is no evidence that Henry James ever subscribed to the notion of a spirit world, he did employ the ghost story genre. The story he used as a basis for the tale of two demonically possessed children and their governess was told to him by a friend and neighbor, Edward

White Benson, then archbishop of Canterbury. While he uses the traditional Gothic setting of a remote and rather sparsely populated country house, James builds suspense by constructing the narrative in such a way that there are no real facts, only the remembered impressions of a woman who has since died, as have the children. There are no living witnesses, no way to get at the truth, only the word of a narrator who swears to the integrity of his source. When the story ends, we don't know if the governess imagined everything, or if the events she described really did happen. Most readers, I am sure, are inclined to believe the story, as James has skillfully managed for it to be told, and thus in the existence of the ghosts who took the children. What intrigues and amuses me is that *The Turn of the Screw* is a work of fiction written by the brother of a practicing spiritualist, based on a story told by the head of the Anglican Church, and narrated by a man devoted to the truth of the tale he is telling. Meanwhile the author, Henry James, held his own cards close to his vest.[4]

While viewing the psychic community with a somewhat jaundiced eye, I resolved to continue to gather and evaluate their insights. I had no choice. But in doing so, I also needed to banish Doyle and become more like Sherlock. So much was fuzzy and equivocal, including my own shifting fancies. I needed Holmes's detachment and his beady eye. I also needed to dig deeper into evidence provided by the scientific community. I might end up concluding that the whole ghost project had been a fool's errand, but I might also console myself with the knowledge of how vast and inscrutable my subject really was.

CHAPTER TWELVE

❧

NOT WHAT I EXPECTED:
A MEETING AT THE
GHOST CLUB

Periodically I receive emails from the Ghost Club, announcing outings or the agenda for monthly meetings. I've always wanted to attend one, both to hear the featured speaker and to size up the membership, to observe the British citizens who carry on the good work begun by William James, Arthur Conan Doyle, and Edward White Benson, archbishop of Canterbury.

Finally we scheduled a trip that would put us in London on the Saturday of a meeting. Don and I would be driving in from the country early that morning, and we agreed that we would go our separate ways, which was fine with him, as he likes to combine culture and exercise by walking to some distant art location, like the Tate Britain on Millbank or the galleries in Hoxton Square. It was chilly and damp on May 15, and, wanting to blend in, I decided to dress conservatively: black flats, gray slacks, and my new black Barbour jacket, the same one I'd seen all over London.

I took the tube from our hotel in Knightsbridge to Marble Arch and emerged from the depths of the subway into a crowd of adolescents, youngsters in various degrees of Goth getup, all gray and black, pierced and tattooed, milling around with the pigeons on the littered square. I wended my way through them, crossed Oxford Street, and walked the several blocks to the Victory Services Club, where the Ghost Club rented space for its events.

I had scouted the location on an earlier London trip. Harboring a romantic notion that any club founded in London in 1862 by prominent members of the arts and sciences would be, well, like a London club, I envisioned wood-paneled rooms, windows draped in maroon velvet, perhaps a butler hovering about with a silver tray. It wasn't a Bertie Woosterish club I imagined, but something more like the Boston Athenaeum, with lots of open bookshelves and journal-strewn tables. It might be a place where I could drop in after shopping at Selfridges and sip a sherry while perusing the latest issue of the *Ghost Club Journal.* After all, I was a member.

When I found the Victory Services Club, on a nondescript road just behind Oxford Street, it proved to be an austere edifice with the generic institutional façade of a town post office or utility company headquarters. I was greeted—*accosted* would be a more apt term—by a uniformed guard who wanted to know what I was doing there. "I am looking for the Ghost Club," I told him, and he frowned. "They only rent a room here one Saturday a month," he said primly. "There isn't a meeting today." His expression and tone said, "And you can leave now." I did.

Later I looked up the Victory Services Club and learned that it is a nonprofit organization for retired and active members of the armed services (unique among London military clubs in that it welcomes all services and all ranks), and that it provides not only a meeting place but dining and accommodations. On my second visit I knew what to expect, then, or so I thought. I anticipated a small auditorium where I could slip into a chair quietly, arriving just as the meeting was due to start; I didn't want to draw attention to myself, a stranger, in what must be a tight group of ghost aficionados familiar to one another.

Again, I was stopped at the entrance and then directed to a conference room on the second floor. The room itself was easy to find, as people were clumped outside trying to crowd into it, and there was a loud buzz of conversation. A young man carrying several folding chairs was trying to penetrate the doorway. I followed him. It was like following in the wake of an ambulance, taking advantage of a clear pathway before others realized they could pull back into the lane. He began setting out the chairs near the front of the room and I sat in one of them, in the third row between a middle-aged woman and a young man who had followed me up the center of the narrow room.

There was a lot of milling about, and I scanned the room, which I estimated was stuffed with between fifty and sixty people. No one paid any attention to me; the woman on my left chatted with a woman in front of her while her husband rifled through some reading material. The young man on my right stowed his knapsack under his chair and sat slouched, arms folded, his demeanor that of one who is anxious for the proceedings to proceed. And it was time, two o'clock. Up front several people were maneuvering a screen into position while a man in a business suit, who I presumed was the club's president, and another man in more casual dress stood chatting. I continued to look about and was surprised at how diverse and how normal-looking the people in the audience were. Yes, they were almost all white, but there was a range of ages, with many young people, as many men as women, everyone dressed pretty much as I was. Yes, there were some gypsyish-looking women with clanking bracelets, a very overweight man whose gray hair was braided down his back, and a couple of young men in Goth attire, but mostly they reminded me of the crowd I see at antique auctions, people who came from all over but who knew each other in this one context.

The speaker was the Reverend Lionel Fanthorpe, an ordained Anglican priest whose pastoral activity seemed to be limited to doing exorcisms and funerals. He was introduced as the author or coauthor of at least two hundred books, short stories, and novels in the science fiction–paranormal genre, and from 1997 to 1998 he had hosted a paranormal documentary series on British television. In addition, I learned later, Fanthorpe was a member of Mensa and a karate instructor.

A stout, balding man with a goatee, the Rev. Fanthorpe was without clerical collar, being dressed in a dark suit, shirt, and tie; he was described in a subsequent journal account as "a twinkle-eyed ball of enthusiasm, over seventy-eight years old!" His topic was "Ghosts and Fivefold Phenomena," but before he began the formal lecture and slide presentation, Rev. Fanthorpe related two personal experiences. The first had occurred during a tour of the catacombs in Rome: he felt a hand descend on his shoulder and turned to see a tall, black-clad figure in a conical hat. The figure looked at him, seeming more curious than threatening. Fanthorpe, who fled the scene, described the figure to Italian friends. They identified the costume as that of funereal priests from two thousand years earlier.

More intriguing from my point of view was the second anecdote, which featured Fanthorpe's old and dear friend Billy. In middle age, Billy had contracted a "terminal disease," no doubt a fast-moving cancer, and died soon thereafter. Fanthorpe was informed of the death by Billy's local priest, and the two clerics began to plan Billy's funeral service.

Soon afterward, while Rev. Fanthorpe was sitting at his desk at home, Billy appeared before him, "looking as he had looked thirty years before," said Fanthorpe. "He looked radiantly happy and said he had a message for me to convey to the priest with whom I was planning his funeral. 'Tell him,' Bill said, 'it was just as Sister Mary Agnes said. All shall be well.'" When Fanthorpe repeated this message to his colleague, the man's jaw dropped. "This is something you couldn't have known. When Bill was dying, I told him about Sister Mary Agnes, how she had assured me as she was dying that, in her words, 'All shall be well.' There is no way you could have known these final words of hers!"

I was writing as fast as I could, hoping no one would find my note-taking odd, since I was the only one doing so. The woman on my left was engrossed in Fanthorpe's remarks, smiling all the while he talked. On my right the young man was shaking his head from time to time, but just barely. Fanthorpe began his lecture, showing slides from a collection he and his wife had made over the years. With the screen and the cassette and the slightly out-of-focus images, it seemed very old-fashioned and very homemade, which of course it was. The five categories of paranormal phenomena were (1) spirits of the dead that appear to the living, as in Hamlet's father; (2) "time slips," in which people disappeared and reappeared without, apparently, knowing they had been gone, which I found confusing, and the example given didn't help: A man went into a public toilet and disappeared for two hours while his wife waited and then sent people in looking for him. They couldn't find him, but then he appeared, not realizing he had been gone for more than a few minutes; the man reported that he had seen strange, futuristic cars, which implied that he had traveled forward in time; (3) parallel universes, in which life may be perceived as being lived in another world. I couldn't grasp this one either, particularly since it included hybrid human-animals; (4) psychic recordings, which refer to the reading and interpretation of emotions etched in the fabric of a building or place; and (5) mental phenomena, such as hallucinations.

For me, category 4, "psychic recordings," offered the greatest possibility for elucidation. This category seemed to describe the kind of presence I'd felt in certain locations, such as in George Sand's house, or even my own, when I'd thought I heard foot-steps on the staircase or a door closing upstairs, which might result from some energy left by former occupants. His comments on mental phenomena resonated as well, for unlike Dr. Sacks and his very specific neurological diagnoses, Fanthorpe asked instead if we had thought, not about the brain's malfunctioning, but about the brain's potential. Certain people, musicians for exam-ple, have a particularly acute sense of hearing. He talked about dowsers, those rare individuals who are able to use a stick or rod to find underground sources of water. "There is hidden power in the human mind," was the gist of Fanthorpe's message. "What can the brain do? We are using only a small part of it. Each of us has infinite power." Here I agreed with Rev. Fanthorpe, having read enough about the topography and functioning of the brain by now to suspect that most people, with guidance and practice, could develop a much broader range of perception, much as we are, even at an advanced age, being coached into greater physi-cal prowess, able even to run marathons.

Later I looked up *astral travel*, wondering if *time slips* might be the same thing, and in fact they do appear to be different terms for the same psychic experience of going into a trance and travel-ing into another, distant time zone. Medium Rosemary Altea, for example, reports having traveled back in time to a Victorian-era village, where she wandered about for a time, apparently unnoticed by the villagers.

During a brief question-and-answer period, someone asked the obvious question. "As an Anglican cleric, how are you perceived? Are there many like you?" Fanthorpe responded that, while more traditional clergy "don't go near it," he and his more progressive colleagues did exorcisms and explored the paranormal because they were both curious and convinced that it was healthier to keep an open mind. This philosophy, he added, was not at odds with his belief in God, and that "He is benign."

The lecture ended and commencement of a social hour in the downstairs lounge was announced by the club president, Alan Murdie. As chairs scraped and people began to talk and move about, I tried to identify a likely interview subject. Everyone seemed to be engrossed in intense conversation. Toward the back of the room, I spied a young woman who looked as I felt, new to the group, eager to join in, but unsure about how to do so. I approached her just as she was being joined by a young man. When I asked how they happened to be there, both seemed delighted to be asked.

The woman, an attractive blonde, spoke with an eastern European accent, her English tentative but adequate for conversation. Her companion was a pale, solidly built young man with close-cropped reddish hair, mid- to late-thirties; a tinge of a cockney accent was discernable as he spoke, which he did with great enthusiasm. This was their second meeting, and he was there because of his own experience with ghosts. He had lived, he told me, in a flat built on the former site of a garage, a mechanics shop, and people had been doing serious black magic there, even killing small animals. He didn't know any of this when he moved in, but his personal collection of Nazi occult memorabilia was attracting the evil spirits back to their old haunt. A huge figure began appearing in his bedroom at night, a black-clad apparition he referred to as "the Angel of Death." A cloud entered his room and expanded to the width of the ceiling, accompanied by a whooshing sound and the smell of petrol. He was terrified but couldn't afford to move, and so he called in an exorcist. But the demons remained. Finally he was able to sell the flat and leave.

Wanting to ask questions and take notes, I suggested that we go for a drink. Downstairs we found a table in an unoccupied corner of the lounge, which was startlingly contemporary in its décor, with chrome and glass tables, angular leather chairs, and a cool blue-gray color scheme—rather like an upscale airport lounge. Once seated, I introduced myself and asked their names—Greta and Andrew. I listened to Andrew retell his story while I took notes and sipped bad white wine.

He told his story eagerly, but without humor or inflection, repeating exactly what he had told me upstairs, not pausing for effect, just seeming to want to get out all of it, all the facts of his experience, each demon and apparition accounted for. It was as if the telling were a proof, or an exorcism. His intensity was tempered when he paused, finally, in order to repeat details when I was finally able to get a word in edgewise and ask for them.

An obvious question: Why did he have Nazi occult memorabilia, and what did it consist of? Nazis, he replied, pursued any path that might further their goals, and investigation of the occult and its potential for domination was among them. He also had some posters of mystical Egyptian figures. What his collection consisted of was not revealed, and I found myself unwilling to pursue this strain of conversation. Later I learned that, due to several authors' well-known speculations on Nazi interest in a racist occult movement called Ariosophy, the idea that Hitler and his henchmen were controlled by a hidden power became popular and widespread. It appeared to me, after I later punched in "Nazi occultism" on Wikipedia, that entire college courses, if not PhD theses, could be built on the subject, so many books had been written. And so, however unpalatable and weird it seemed to me, Andrew's collecting of Nazi occult material was not unusual.

Yet as he talked, I was reminded of a man my husband and I had met years earlier when we were looking at houses in rural Massachusetts. The house was a vintage frame colonial, in perfect period condition, but chockablock with not very colonial objects, such as mirrored balls, daggers, astrology charts, and panels and posters with geometric symbols. A small greenhouse off the kitchen was stocked with plants that I, an ardent gardener, did not recognize. The owner, who appeared to live in the house alone, was eager to show us about, explaining that he was moving to Hamburg, Germany. He had had many lookers but no takers and couldn't understand why. As we stood in an upstairs bedroom, gazing down at a dresser top that held a display of a white silk scarf draped carefully over something spherical, with a dagger positioned just in front of it, centered and parallel to the dresser's edge, I got a chill, a strong sense of menace, and felt a need to get out of the house as quickly as possible. Perhaps Andrew had been living in a place with the same menacing energy of a former occupant.

What did he do for work? I asked, anxious to leave the Nazis. He worked for an import-export firm at Heathrow but was also a writer. I could read his novel on Amazon Kindle.

The crowd in the lounge had dispersed, and I decided it was time to leave, having missed my chance to interview other Ghost Club members. Greta, who had mostly just smiled and looked on while Andrew talked, perked up when I said I was from Boston. "Oh, I may be going there soon!" she exclaimed. "My sister is moving there. It is fate that you are here!"

We said good-bye, and I left them, promising to search out Andrew's novel *The Armour of Light*.

I'd spent most of a London afternoon at the Ghost Club, forsaking a trip to the National Gallery or shopping in Harvey Nichols, for Rev. Fanthorpe's lecture and a conversation with someone whose ghost experience was on the very bizarre end of the scale. What had I learned? Not much that was new, beyond finding another flourishing subculture, Nazi occult–memorabilia devotees. Andrew's account of demon spirits was true, perhaps, and the Reverend Fanthorpe's post-death visit from Billy seemed to constitute evidence of spirit life. But why couldn't his friend Billy have appeared to the other priest himself, and saved Fanthorpe the trouble of having to convey the message?

Because he was a prominent media personality, I found ample material on Fanthorpe when I returned home and began searching for it. In 2012 he had given a TEDx talk, during which he reviewed well-known unsolved mysteries, some quite ancient, which he had revisited in order to discover whether or not there was a rational explanation for seemingly inexplicable events. Using various historical documents and records, as well as on-site research, Fanthorpe picked and poked his way through all kinds of data to conclude that accepted accounts of various events were false, that they were based on first impressions, assumptions, and superstitions—and he then used solid information and common sense to deduce, much like Sherlock Holmes, what really happened. (One Victorian-era tale involved the discovery and dismembering of the corpse of an alleged vampire, because blood had been found on the tomb of someone long dead; Fanthorpe was able to identify the true source of the blood, a mental patient who had been badly injured and taken refuge in the rural chapel, getting blood everywhere before moving on and later dying of his wound.)

I felt disappointed after the meeting, and wasn't quite sure why, other than that there had been a distinct lack of butlers serving sherry on silver trays. I had heard two first-person accounts of ghost encounters. And I had gleaned some new information from Fanthorpe's lecture. But Andrew's story was so bizarre that I found myself thinking about where it would fit in Oliver Sacks's book *Hallucinations*. And Fanthorpe had so emphasized the skeptic's point of view, with his years of debunking old ghost stories, that even though he stressed his visit from the deceased Billy as proof of afterlife, I couldn't be sure where he really stood with respect to ghosts.

CHAPTER THIRTEEN

✵

SCIENCE LESSONS

One of my fellow board members at MIT's List Art Center is a faculty member who won the Nobel Prize in physics in 1990. He is an affable man who considered an art career before choosing to study mathematics at the University of Chicago, and I felt comfortable telling him about the goings-on in my house and asking him why, given the range of topics under study at MIT, no research was being done on the paranormal. "There's no money in it," he told me, deflecting my question in a nonjudgmental way I understood and appreciated. Yet lack of funding was no doubt one of the reasons so few scientists, save those involved in parapsychology, had investigated the small-scale, domestic occurrences that provide mysteries as intriguing in their way as black holes. (One exception was the substantial investment in the study of ESP made by the US government and large corporations during the 1950s, when the Cold War had to be won, and mind control was thought to have potential as a defensive weapon.)

Knowing that if I was to be thorough, I must eventually seek an explanation for events in my house that did not involve ghosts, I have, while exploring the new and fascinating world of the paranormal, also read and clipped materials on science subjects that seem relevant, most often articles and book reviews on developments in neuroscience and cosmology. I diligently scan the Tuesday Science Times section in the *New York Times*, as well as any reviews of books dealing with neuroscience, stuffing clippings and magazine pages into an outsize manila envelope that I have labeled "Science" in thick black marker. But once an article has been skimmed, clipped, and stuffed into the envelope, I promptly forget about it. It isn't just that science is not as much fun as the paranormal, it's that the field of science is intimidating. As a liberal arts major in college, I was required to take only one science course and chose biology. The lingua franca of science is mathematics and I last encountered math—geometry—in my sophomore year of high school. My post-college reading has been mostly novels and art history, and unlike reviews of a play I may eventually see or a book I might read, articles featuring new developments in science are not ones I am likely to pursue or even discuss. Neurology, cosmology, quantum physics—these are states in a very foreign country.

The articles I do tend to remember are those dealing with neuroscience, because what I really have been looking for is reinforcement of phenomena related to the paranormal. I hoped to find some published evidence of the human brain's capability for telepathic or clairvoyant perception, any inkling that we all may have a latent ability resembling the "sixth sense" claimed by mediums, spiritualists, and other denizens of the paranormal world. Unhappily I have discovered only that brain science is in its early stages, but more significantly that the world of science views the world of the supernatural with disdain, if it views it at all. Oliver Sacks, whose case studies of hallucinations bothered me because of his insistence on crediting all "otherworldly" experience to a kink in the neurological system, represented a bias I found typical. For example, when Dr. Daryl Bem of Cornell presented findings that seemed to prove that human beings do possess something resembling extrasensory perception, or ESP, he was promptly discredited by colleagues in his field. Earlier studies on psychical subjects had been done at Duke and Stanford universities, and a major research effort continues at the Society for Psychical Research in London. However, I also learned that the scientific community was at odds with these efforts. In the US, research projects related to ESP have been dropped or discredited, as both researchers and funders debate whether this is a valid or useful area of study.

And Bem wasn't even concerned with paranormal subjects, only with an inquiry into the powers of the human mind and whether or not "foresight" is more about sensory perception than judgment. Something about ghosts, ESP, and other intimations of afterlife seems to put people off. Is it an unwillingness to confront mortality? Even among those scientists able to reconcile their scientific work with religious beliefs that may include life after death, a derisive attitude prevails when paranormal subjects are raised. As I read about Bem's experience, I had felt increasingly annoyed on his behalf: a social psychologist who did graduate work in physics at MIT, Bem was an emeritus professor with a long and distinguished career. During the years when I was writing case studies for the Organizational Behavior Department at Harvard Business School, there was tension between faculty promoting the need for study of psychology-based techniques of management and professors of more traditional subjects—finance, marketing, production— who believed that the proper concern of business students was learning how to make and sell things. (Students were even more dismissive, joking that the cases I wrote were about where to put the watercooler.) Was the scientific community's disdainful posture similarly myopic and territorial, allowing physicists and biologists, who deal in observable, quantifiable phenomena, to barricade themselves against incursions by psychologists, sociologists, theologians, and the like?

Partially. But I decided that their resistance might also be due to a common human tendency to avoid dealing with the inscrutable. In a *New York Times* editorial titled "When Things Happen That You Can't Explain," T. M. Luhrmann, an anthropologist, described his own and several other peoples' inexplicable experiences.[1]

Luhrmann began with an event that occurred in England when he was twenty-three and doing research on practicing magicians, a British subculture with unique customs. "I was sitting in a commuter train to London the first time I felt supernatural power rip through me," Luhrmann wrote, immersed at the time in a text by an "adept," a figure of significant power for magicians. Trying to mentally identify with the adept's ability to transmit "forces from a higher spiritual reality," Luhrmann suddenly felt intense inner power and a heightened sense of awareness. "And then wisps of smoke came out of my backpack, where I had tossed my bicycle lights. One of them was melting."

Wow! I thought. *This is amazing!* Anticipating further astonishing developments, I was disappointed and puzzled when Luhrmann skipped immediately to examples of other people's inexplicable experiences, commenting that, "Sometimes people . . . tuck them away as events they can't explain." "I never did figure out what was going on with those bicycle lights," Luhrmann finished.

What? I reread the article, baffled by the inconclusiveness of this account. The other examples concerned people who had felt versions of the same sense of power, much like what journalist

Barbara Ehrenreich describes in her book, *Living with a Wild God.* "Something poured into me and I poured out into it," she writes in "A Rationalist's Mystical Moment."[2] These experiences are subjective and can reasonably be viewed as possible hallucinations. But the melting bicycle light was an observable event. How could anyone discount a bicycle light that *melted*, just shrug their shoulders and turn away?

I decided to Google the author, wanting to know if he had any chops as a researcher, any evidence of an enquiring mind. The first thing I learned was that T. M. Luhrmann was a woman, Tanya Marie Luhrmann, a Stanford professor who writes about how people experience God and the supernatural, "people" including modern-day witches, charismatic Christians, Indian Parsis, and psychiatric residents. What I read about her research and publications seemed to me to indicate a scholar who regarded her subjects' experiences as cultural and social phenomena, not supernatural ones. No doubt her own experience had been safely filed away with other ethnographic curiosities.

Such a missed opportunity, I thought; Tanya Marie could have discovered something far more intriguing if she had permitted herself a detour. I had to admit that if it had been only the hairbrush that moved, I might have just let the question of "how" go unanswered, too. But there were those other incidents, the piano playing itself and Dan's shove on the stairs, and I had become like a dog with a bone, unable to let it go.

My random readings in the popular press didn't seem adequate if I was going to give science a fair chance at providing an alternative explanation for my own inexplicable experience. But how was I to get my aged, English major's mind around current scientific concepts? The mother of one of my daughter's friends, a PhD in biology who taught at Boston University, once said that she feared people with rudimentary science educations were increasingly unlikely to be able to understand or assess much that was happening in the world. Clearly I was proof of this, having taken only one biology course decades earlier, and I had dozed through much of that because the large lecture class was taught right after lunch. Now I wanted to get a grasp on physics, which seemed to be the most relevant area of science, given that it dealt with (mostly) material things and how they moved and transformed themselves. When I read reviews of Brian Greene's new book, *The Fabric of the Cosmos*, I bought a copy; in the *New York Times* Janet Maslin had described the author as "a skilled and kindly explicator," which was fine, but it was the blurb from *Entertainment Weekly* that sold me: "If anyone can popularize tough science, it's Greene."[3]

One spring afternoon I sat down at my desk with pad, paper, and Greene's 569-page book. I read the preface, which went pretty well, as it dealt with generalities about space and time; i.e., were they tangible entities or just useful constructs? The first chapter, "Space, Time, and Why Things Are as They Are," also went well; looking back, I find that I underlined this section from page 5: "The overarching lesson that has emerged from scientific inquiry over the last century is that human experience is often a misleading guide to the true nature of reality. Lying just beneath the surface of the everyday is a world we'd hardly recognize. Followers of the occult, devotees of astrology, and those who hold religious principles that speak to a reality beyond experience have . . . long since arrived at a similar conclusion."

Now we're getting somewhere, I thought, but Greene went on to promote the superior value of science in revealing "the true nature of physical reality."

Greene's physical reality seemed to refer to some aspect of particles or black holes, and I was thinking about a much more prosaic reality, ordinary things like hairbrushes and sofas that moved about without human intervention. I also was thinking of what we don't know, or perceive, of the world of the spirit. My lack of an adequate science background, or even vocabulary, rendered the ensuing pages increasingly incomprehensible to me, dealing as they did with electrons and such. I tried to take notes, but my mind kept wandering, and after sixty pages I put the book down, unable to translate the esoteric language and concepts, such as "the relativity of simultaneity." It was as if I had gone out for an exploratory hike in the woods and found myself climbing the face of a cliff, without a guide or proper equipment.

Even some of the articles and reviews I had clipped, supposedly intended for a general reader, included concepts and terms I recognized but did not really understand, like "electromagnetic field." My fear of incomprehension was somewhat offset by my pleasure in discovering that in science, too, uncertainty was a constant—at least, that was my interpretation of articles describing recent developments in neuroscience and cosmology that often concluded with some version of "there is so much we don't yet know." I also realized that, while explanations from the paranormal world suffered from limited sample size, lack of rigorous documentation, and the anecdotal nature of most observed phenomena, scientific investigations, while often occurring over long periods of time and involving thousands of subjects, often yielded similarly ambiguous results.

I was relieved to come across an essay in the *New York Times* that gave some heft to my belief that ghosts and spirits might be part of the great as-yet-unknown. Philip Kitcher, a philosophy professor critiquing a book titled *The Atheist's Guide to Reality*, credited science with increasing our ability to perceive (via such inventions as the microscope), while also crediting thinkers from a range of fields with the ability to build upon this enhanced perception and "to go much further."[4] Yes, I thought. We may be on a vast learning curve, with much more both to know, and to un-know. The earth is not flat. The sun does not move. And ghosts may be with us, whether we see them or not. And as I kept my science radar on while reading outside the field, I began to notice that artists, too, were absorbed with the unknown. "Explain consciousness," a young female character asks of her tutor in Tom Stoppard's play *The Hard Problem*. Exactly.[5]

I also read a review of a new documentary, *Particle Fever*, that featured CERN (the European Center for Nuclear Research) and the scientists most involved in the search for the Higgs boson.[6] The *New York Times* had offered a multi-page, user-friendly guide to this quest some months earlier, but for me the article was a soporific even more powerful than post-lunch biology lectures. The whole business was so abstract, the concepts and scientific terms so unfamiliar, there was nothing I could picture or relate to any aspect of my personal experience. Movie critic A. O. Scott described *Particle Fever* as a "mind-blowing documentary," and while by now I had no illusions as to my ability to comprehend what people like Scott might find "accessible," I thought I might benefit from being forced to hear scientists talk about their work for two hours. And so I spent a late weekday afternoon in the Coolidge Theater in Brookline, where *Particle Fever* was showing in the small, twenty-four-seat upstairs theater. The twenty-three other people in attendance I judged to be members of the physics community, perhaps a contingent from MIT, as they all seemed to be together, chatting amiably and passing bags of popcorn back and forth.

The film was a revelation. Many people involved in the Higgs project were interviewed, but the ones who impressed me were the younger people, so thoroughly engaged in and excited about the prospect of discovering this subatomic particle. A young scientist from Princeton, Nima Arkani-Hamed, was both exceptionally attractive and articulate. He described his work in between writing cryptic (to me) formulas on the blackboard and playing table tennis. Monica Dunford, an applied physicist from California, explained the difference between her interests and those of the theoretical physicists while riding her bicycle to work. CERN's administrative head, Fabiola Gianotti, had trained as a classical pianist; her demeanor was both graceful and businesslike, and I loved that she was wearing a bright red dress and serious jewelry. All of these scientists, some of the most prominent in their fields, were palpably excited to be involved in the project, particularly as they grew closer to the day of discovery. While I still can't tell you what a boson is, I did understand, after listening to a dozen physicists emote, that what was at stake was a fundamental difference in theories about the nature of the universe. Our universe was either "supersymmetrical," pretty much as how we now perceive it, at the center of a constellation, or it was part of a chaotic "multiverse," only one of many universes. (Some months later the results were in, and option two, our being part of a multiverse, appeared to be likely.)

It seemed to me that while scientists might choose to scoff at the notion of afterlife, and certainly at the belief that God made the world, what they were contemplating as possible was a reality far more dumbfounding than anything put forth by creationists. Our own world, the eons of culture that had developed on planet Earth, would be insignificant within the context of a multiverse. Aliens, who might or might not resemble E.T., would have to be assumed as quite possibly having cultures and knowledge far more advanced than our own.

CERN and the Higgs project involved thousands of people and billions of dollars. But because there was "no money in it," as my MIT friend had told me, research into paranormal phenomena was stuck at a very primitive stage and likely to remain there. Whether trying to prove the existence of the Loch Ness Monster or the Higgs boson, only a documented sighting is acceptable evidence, and documented sightings, in the scientific world and particularly in the paranormal one, are hard to come by. People who believe in spirit life believe, for the most part, in what they see or experience or choose to believe, and none of this passes for proof. Much as I wanted to poke holes in Oliver Sacks's contention that it was all about the brain, I couldn't accept Eben Alexander's near-death experience as proof of afterlife, either. Dr. Alexander was all by himself when he went to heaven and back, and he didn't take any pictures.

What I was discovering, as I did my science homework, was that science was unlikely to have an explanation for me. Any scientific explanation might be no more definitive than those offered by the medium Echo Bodine or by the psychic Lorraine with her tarot cards. And while practitioners in the paranormal professions are often, and legitimately, accused of fraud, so are those working in the field of science. During the past year, I had come across several articles on scientists who had been discredited for falsifying their data (one researcher had fabricated an entire nine-hundred-patient study published in the *Lancet*). For scientists, the gold standard is whether or not their research results can be replicated; that is, whether the same tests can be repeated again and again with identical results. In the paranormal world, conversely, consistent duplication by mediums is more likely to signal deceit, as spirits are reputed to be quixotic in their behavior.

More to the point, where neuroscience is concerned, it seems to me that it is early days. The brain and consciousness are nowhere near being comprehended, despite the claims of those scientists who say they do understand, that there is no more to the mind and consciousness than neurons, and what we see through the microscope is what we get. The question remains, as stated by Stoppard's character, "Explain consciousness." These people really do not know yet what they are talking about. "The truth is that we are still at a loss to explain how the brain does all but the most elementary things," Gary Marcus, a New York University psychologist wrote recently in a collection of essays.[7] My daughter, a physician and faculty member at Brown University, called me as I was writing this; she suffers from migraines and was on her way to have acupuncture, the only treatment that has helped her. "Why does it work?" I asked her. "Who knows?" she replied.

Two aspects of our experienced world now seem to me, science dilettante that I am, relevant to the issue of afterlife and thus to the possible existence of ghosts, or spirits. One is energy and the other is consciousness. Energy, I have learned, cannot be created or destroyed, only transferred or transformed, as when the energy from the sun is used by plants to grow and is then cast off as water and carbon dioxide. Consciousness is either some mechanical function of the brain that has not yet been identified and parsed, or—and this is major—*it is an entirely different phenomenon, the mind separate from the brain, the life-giving spirit a quality that exists above and beyond our physical being.*

Here is where I recall all the mediums I have studied—Echo Bodine and Lorraine and Rosemary Altea—every one equating spirits with energy, energy which they in turn may absorb or transfer from living humans or which is simply felt by those able to perceive it. If in fact our minds are a super potent form of energy, how is this energy recycled once it leaves the body?

Well, so far as I know, no one in the scientific community is asking this question, tantalizing as it is. That is, no one except Dr. Jim Tucker, a child psychiatrist at the University of Virginia, who has spent fifteen years studying children who have memories from a past life. I learned about Dr. Tucker from the spring

2017 *Ghost Club Journal,* and went straight to Wikipedia and other sources to learn whether Tucker was legitimate or a possible wacko. He is legit. I ended up spending an hour hunched over my laptop watching a YouTube video about a Scottish boy who remembers a past life lived on an island in the Hebrides. Tucker had gone to interview the boy, Cameron Macaulay, and his mother, and to escort them to the island where Cameron claimed to have lived.

The mother's Glaswegian accent was thick, the little boy kept jumping and leaping over furniture while he talked, and Tucker himself is very soft-spoken, so I had difficulty hearing everything. But the gist was that Cameron remembered living in a white house near the sea, and he could see the water from his window, as well as small planes landing on the nearby beach. He referred to his mother, whom he missed terribly, and brothers and sisters, and said that his father, last name Robertson, had died when a car hit him.

Once on the island they discovered that a family named Robertson had once lived there; arriving at the former Robertson address, the topography was as Cameron had described it. Cameron became very quiet when they entered the house, clinging to his mother and looking distressed. Subsequent research confirmed the father's death but not the existence of children. The video included segments of an attractive brown-haired woman in a red bathing suit, presumably Mrs. Robertson. Cameron later would dwell on his fondness for his former mother, whom he professed to miss greatly, although these feelings did not interfere with his attachment to his real mother. (I concluded that the feeling of loss Cameron felt for his former "mother" was really the bereavement of a husband who had lost his wife, and the mother-child, husband-wife relationship had been somehow transposed in this particular reincarnation.)

According to Dr. Tucker, Cameron is representative of twenty-five hundred children he has studied who claim to have memories of previous lives, many of which he has tracked and verified. Typically, the people reincarnated in these children have died a sudden and/or unnatural death, and there is a lapse on average of sixteen months between their death and the birth of a child host. These memories remain vivid for the child until about age six or seven, when they subside, and the child proceeds to live with its own discrete identity.

Dr. Tucker refers to quantum physics and the idea that our souls exist as energy on a subatomic level, and that the soul—or mind—can exist separately from our bodies. "In these cases," Tucker is quoted as saying, "it seems—at least on the face of it—that a consciousness has then become attached to a new brain, and has shown up as past life memories."[8] This was radical stuff, a bit more than I bargained for, and after watching the video, I felt almost like filing it with Professor Luhrmann's curiosities, because I just couldn't process the idea of these children being vessels for the memories of dead people. It seemed too great a burden, too much of an imposition, to superimpose an alien identity upon a helpless child, to say nothing of their families.

Yet my review of the clippings I had saved and underlined, while not based on the kind of clinical experience that Tucker has, revealed a consistent thread of dissent regarding the position of neuroscience that there is no such thing as a discrete mind. I found an essay by Edward Frenkel, professor of mathematics at UC Berkeley, "The Reality of Quantum Weirdness." Frenkel begins with a reference to *Rashomon*, Akira Kurosawa's film about three perceptions of the same event, asking which version is true. Frenkel extrapolates to ask more complex questions. "Is there a true story, or is our belief in a definite, objective, observer-independent reality an illusion? . . . Is there a fixed reality apart from our various observations of it? Or is reality nothing more than a kaleidoscope of infinite possibilities?" He, too, is concerned with quantum physics and the mutability of particles, but concludes that we should "regard the paradoxes of quantum physics as a metaphor for the unknown infinite possibilities of our own existence."[9]

While I was befuddled by much of Frenkel's argument, dealing as it did with electrons and particles and waves, it was easy to get the gist. The world is more complicated and inscrutable than we like to think. And it occurred to me, as I tried to absorb Frenkel's argument, that what science does is figure out enough about the physical world to make use of it, that is, to make light bulbs light up, planes fly, and bombs explode. It does a poor job of less tangible chores, such as explaining consciousness, afterlife, or even why bicycle lights melt and hairbrushes disappear.

While investigators of haunted houses mostly sit around waiting for something to happen, and then try to capture a fuzzy image, scientific investigators create elaborate artificial situations with hundreds of subjects, plan and execute experiments with exquisite precision, and often wonder what it is that they have seen and what it might mean. Just recently I read about an MIT-generated experiment called LIGO (Laser Interferometer Gravitational-wave Observatory), now an elaborate facility with two-and-a-half-mile vacuum tubes housing lasers and mirrors, that recently detected new gravity waves resulting from a collision of black holes billions of light-years ago. But all this tells us, according to a data analyst, is that there are a lot of black holes out there. The paranormal investigators' methods and equipment may be crude, but the outcomes are often very similar: partial answers, ambiguous results. Proof of something, but what?

And science is, like most professional fields, riddled with blindness and territorial concerns, which have until recently rendered practices like acupuncture and its adherents marginal at best. Even in *Particle Fever*, the divide between those who were invested in the concept of multiverses and those who were not was obvious, at times as absolute and acrimonious as the current rift between Democrats and Republicans. Others look for other ways to discredit research results they find noxious. In the case of Dr. Bem, a colleague, who rejected his ESP results but professed to have the highest respect for Bem's integrity and adherence to accepted research methodology, decided that it was the methodology that was at fault. In a May 17, 2017, *Slate* cover story, "Daryl Bem Proved ESP Is Real, Which Means Science Is Broken," Daniel Engber reports on a major rethinking of research methods within the social sciences. A prominent European researcher had been stunned by the realization that Bem's research was flawless, meaning that the flaw was in the methodology, which apparently could be used to prove almost anything. Bem's findings were "methodologically sound and logically insane."[10]

I found no answers but a good deal of comfort and good sense in the words of the most endearing and thoughtful of the scientists I met in print, Guy Consolmagno. Introduced by Dennis Overbye in the Science section of the *New York Times*, Brother Consolmagno, as he is known at the Vatican Observatory, an MIT graduate, spent ten years as a planetary scientist specializing in meteorites before joining the Jesuits. Overbye had contacted him for a Christmas-season piece regarding a question about potential inhabitants of other planets. How might God treat aliens with respect to salvation? Was Jesus born to save them, too, or must they have their own gods? Brother Consolmagno replied that Christmas for aliens could be a wonderful story, but that he didn't have any answers and that was part of the fun. "Contrary to popular perception . . . religion, unlike science, is not a closed book. Science is stuff we understand about truths we only partially grasp. Religion is trying to get closer to the truths we don't understand. The more you know, the more you know you don't understand. That's called progress."[11]

Carlo Rovelli, an Italian theoretical physicist and author of *Seven Brief Lessons on Physics*, offered another kind of comfort. While concurring that new mysteries are a constant in scientific practice, Rovelli also observes that we are a naturally curious species and that Einstein himself continued to test his own work and to understand more, debating for years with Niels Bohr over new ideas that challenged his own. "Our desire for knowledge burns," Rovelli writes. "Here, on the edge of what we know . . . shines the mystery and beauty of the world. And it's breathtaking."[12] After reading Rovelli's eighty-one-page work, my frustration with science dissipated, as I understood that it was about the message, not the often-myopic messengers. The more generous and philosophical of science practitioners offer an admission that, if I may paraphrase scripture, the natural world works in mysterious ways its wonders to perform.

CHAPTER FOURTEEN

CANDIDATES FOR RESIDENT GHOST(S)

When I first visited the psychic Lorraine and posed my question about whether a ghost was living in our house, she told me that we definitely had a "portal" through which spirits were entering. I was to avoid using spirit-attracting devices such as a Ouija board because I'd likely attract a number of neighborhood ghosts with no connection to me or my house–rather, I thought, like the Japanese beetle traps I once put up in my garden, only to find that the bait lured the rose-eating pests from yards far beyond my own.

While Lorraine had been wrong about a number of things, she was right about the influx of spirits. Except that the portal through which they wafted was not a paranormal one; it was my computer screen, where deceased former residents suddenly commenced entering via new blog postings and websites. Eventually the pool of candidates for resident ghost would grow well beyond the few I already knew about.

Years earlier, wanting to know what our 1875 house looked like before major alterations in 1917, and in particular where the original front door had been, I had gone to Boston's Department of Inspectional Services, where building permits are issued and stored. The halls were clogged with pacing contractors waiting for permission to implement various repairs and renovations, and I assumed a long wait. I found the appropriate clerk and stated my business, then retired to lean against the wall with several other applicants. I was surprised to be summoned to the counter several minutes later. Expecting a heavy carton of documents, I was instead presented with a letter-size envelope. Inside I found the original building permit, dated April 1875, identifying the owner as C. P. Putnam and the architect as J. Pickering Putnam.

The architect's firm had closed in the early 1920s, and I was unable to find any record of his design; examination of materials in the archives of the Boston Historic Society and of volumes devoted to Boston architecture produced numerous early Back Bay street scenes, but none that included our house. I thought that if I could identify the owner, I might find some clue, or even a family photo, that might reveal the original location of the front door, and so I set out to identify "C. P. Putnam."

Putnam is a prominent name in Boston, associated with a major financial institution as well as members of the city's most elite social class. But who was C. P. Putnam? I had been a desultory user of library reference services in college, and now, so many years later, I had to acquaint myself with the Boston Public Library's systems and collections, as well as learn how to use them. I finally mastered the crotchety microfilm machines and scrolled through yards of coiled negatives, eventually learning from census records that Putnam was still living in the house in 1900; a Lucy Putnam assumed ownership in 1916. Thinking that C. P. must have died about this time, I went to the *New York Times* and the *Boston Globe* for obituaries, where I found C. P. Putnam remembered on April 15, 1914. "A noted specialist in diseases of children," Charles Pickering Putnam had been a prominent pediatrician and philanthropist, the grandson of the founder of Massachusetts General Hospital, and a dedicated public servant who was at the time of his death the president of Boston Associated Charities. He was survived by his wife, Lucy, and three children: Charles, Tracy, and Martha. Dr. Putnam, age fifty-nine, had died at home after a brief illness.

Having nearly forgotten how much I once cared about where the front door had been, I decided to revisit this material in an attempt to identify our ghost. I gasped when I read "died at home." Was Charles Pickering Putnam our ghost? An elderly doctor, member of one of Boston's elite families, devoted do-gooder? I'd always envisioned the ghost as a servant, given the laundry folding and bed moving, perhaps a young woman who had died during the 1918 Spanish influenza epidemic. While pleased that our house's first owner was, according to the *Globe*, "a beloved civic figure," I didn't like to think it was Dr. Putnam's beloved spirit residing with us now. I pictured him as a crusty Victorian who would be appalled by our family's indecorous twenty-first-century lifestyle.

Permit records had indicated that the house was next owned by Rudolf (a misspelling of Rudolph) Weld, who in 1917 commissioned major changes, including the addition of a bay window on the third floor, the garden-level entry, and a curved staircase between the first and second floors. But after all of this renovation work, the Welds had decamped ten years later. Why?

Boston has as many Welds as Putnams, "Boston Brahmins" who mostly are descendants of the prerevolutionary ruling class. (The term *Boston Brahmin* was coined by physician and writer

Oliver Wendell Holmes, Sr., in an 1860 issue of the *Atlantic Monthly*; Holmes described Boston's most elite citizens as similar to the highest level of Hindu society, being educated, wealthy, enlightened, and entitled.) While Welds had, by the time of my researches, spread to New York and even New Jersey, the name retains its prominence in Boston, currently identified with White, Weld, a venerable investment company; Weld Boat House at Harvard; and former Massachusetts governor Bill Weld. By the time I began looking for Rudolph Weld, Welds had proliferated to the extent that there were dozens in the Boston-area phone books, some of whom, I suspected, were distant or non-relations. (I was surprised to find the actress Tuesday Weld cited among prominent members of the clan.)

Returning to the microfilm room of the BPL, I used census data to locate the Weld family, which included Rudolph, his wife, Sylvia, and three young daughters. There also were five female servants listed, one each from Sweden, Finland, and Ireland, and two from Massachusetts (no names were given). Mr. Weld was a merchant, a cotton broker, but the name of his firm was blotched and illegible. What I needed next was an obituary to fill in the blanks. But when I finally tracked one down, I learned only that R. Weld had died in August 1941, age fifty-eight, of injuries sustained in an auto accident.

Serendipity came to my aid. I had poked around newspaper files, the Social Register, and Harvard alumni reports, and found no trace, nothing to tell me who the Welds really were. Then one evening when we were hosting a fund-raising event for a local art museum, I began chatting with Eloise Hodges, a woman I'd known for years in her role as director of a foundation that funds local art projects. She had asked about the house, and I told her about my research into its owners, adding that while I had learned quite a bit about the original owner, Rudolph Weld had eluded me. "Oh," she said, laughing, "you must mean Uncle Rudy!" Eloise said she was his great-grandniece and promised to send me a page of material about him.

Her account proved far more colorful than anything I'd found at the library: "Rudolph's father, Stephen, served illustriously in the Civil War and had a very successful career in the cotton business. . . . Stephen left the business to his three surviving sons—Ned, Rudolph, and Philip—but it failed and was sold in 1926."

"It occurs to me," Eloise had written, "that Rudolph and Sylvia, his wife, might have moved out of their house on Marlborough Street around 1926 when the firm was sold and finances were a bit tight. . . . [Rudy] was legendary for his practical jokes, raucous sense of humor and, at times, almost childlike behavior. I heard this could have been due to a fall from a horse while playing polo when he might have suffered some sort of brain damage. . . . He had lots of charm, according to various family members."

Eloise had attached a family tree for that branch of the Weld family. I noted that one of Rudolph's daughters and I shared the same birthday, April 18.

The Welds had sold the house to Dr. and Mrs. Colkert Caner, from whom we bought it fifty years later. We'd had only brief contact with the Caners, and both had died several years after moving; most of what I knew about them came from their extensive obituaries in the *Boston Globe*. Dr. Caner, eighty-nine, had graduated from Harvard and Harvard Medical School and had had a long career as a neurologist and psychiatrist. He was a champion golfer and tennis player, having competed at Wimbledon. He also was a member of Boston's most exclusive clubs, including the Porcellian at Harvard, the Country Club of Brookline, and the Somerset Club. Mrs. Caner, who died the following year, was a graduate of the Presbyterian Hospital School of Nursing at Columbia University. Her interests included the restoration of historic houses and writing and illustrating articles for the *Garden Club of America* magazine. At age seventy-one, she had published a novel set in nineteenth-century Philadelphia, *Time Against the Sky*. They were survived by three children, a son and two daughters.

Now that my search for a front door had been supplanted by a search for ghosts, I was forced to see these earlier families in a different light. I thought about the original owners, the Putnams, and how Dr. Putnam had died in the house. I had to accept Dr. Putnam as a candidate. Perhaps his wife was as well, but, after scouring the obituaries, I learned that she died twelve years later, after moving to a house down the street. I knew nothing about the Putnams' servants, whether any of them had died while living in our house, and there seemed to be no way of finding out, as servants did not even merit a name in the census records.

Then, just as I was mulling over the possibility of cohabiting with one or two elderly Putnams, a new website literally popped up on my computer screen. Wanting to check his date of death, I'd just punched in "Charles Pickering Putnam" and there it was, courtesy of bostonarchitecture.org, a color photo of our house, accompanied by a page and a half of text describing all of its former inhabitants. It was as if our ghost, disgusted with the paucity of the information I had gleaned, had poked me in the back and said, "See, you think you know about everyone who has lived here? Take a look at this!" I learned that Dr. Charles P. Putnam had moved into the newly built house with his brother James Jackson Putnam, and two sisters, Elizabeth Cabot Putnam and Anna Cabot Putnam. Dr. James Jackson Putnam was a physician specializing in neurology. Anna was an artist. Elizabeth was not identified by profession or interest. They all lived together until James married and moved one block away. Then C. P. married Lucy Washburn. About twenty years later, sister Elizabeth, apparently unmarried, moved to a house next door to her brother James. When C. P. died, his widow, Lucy, their three children, and remaining sister, Anna, moved next door to James and Elizabeth, so that three contiguous buildings now housed the entire Putnam family.

While still living in our house, however, the Putnam family had been joined by various other relatives and guests, most notably Madeleine Yale Wynne and her son, who stayed for five years. Madeleine Wynne (the middle name "Yale" refers to the lock family) was a prominent artist; she attended Boston's School of the Museum of Fine Arts and later acquired a reputation for being one of the first women to do large metal sculpture.

As I assessed this growing crowd of candidates for resident ghost, I had to conclude that the elder Putnams were still definite possibilities, although I couldn't picture them hiding hairbrushes or moving beds. Elizabeth Putnam had moved out to be closer to her brother James. Anna Putnam, the spinster sister, was more likely to be attached to our house, where she had lived almost her entire adult life, dying within several years after moving. Perhaps she hadn't wanted to leave; it wasn't clear why the family had moved, although it is likely that economics had something to do with it. Their new home was smaller, and perhaps C. P.'s widow profited from the sale. It was also possible that the new house was configured in a way more congenial to the inclusion of paying guests; I subsequently learned that after James Putnam died, his wife added a lodger to their household. And I now believe that Madeleine Wynne and her son were paying guests, as it seems unlikely, given her family wealth, that they would have come for a visit and stayed five years.

I decided to eliminate the Welds entirely. While "Uncle Rudy" seemed the kind of character whose ghost would play tricks, they had spent only ten years in the house; the three daughters eventually married and moved to other cities.

As for the Caners, despite their obvious qualifications, having lived in the house for fifty years and dying shortly after age and health problems had forced them to move to smaller, single-level quarters, I was uncomfortable with the idea of Caner ghosts hanging about. I had run into them several times walking in the neighborhood—tall, gaunt Dr. Caner with his tweed cap and bow tie, and his much smaller wife, gloved and hatted, her gray hair in a bun—and while both had been extremely pleasant during our chance encounters, the idea that these two elderly souls were still in the house was creepy. But if the ghost was a Putnam, it would have been in residence while the Caners lived here, and one of their children might have information on the subject.

I knew that the Caners' younger daughter, Lila, lived nearby, and I had been meaning to contact her for years with questions about what the house had been like when she and her family lived in it. When I called and introduced myself, she explained that, while she and her husband had just moved to a town north of Boston, she had to come into the city the following day and would be happy to pay me a visit.

The former Lila Caner appeared at my door on a bright July morning, a handsome woman in her early eighties with salt-and-pepper hair. She wore slacks and athletic shoes, and while claiming a concern about her agility and balance, showed no hesitation in climbing the stairs. An artist herself, Lila remarked on the extent of our art collection, saying that her recent move had forced her to rehang forty-five of her own works. We toured the house from top to bottom, and Lila showed me where the door had been between two bedrooms on the fourth floor; a swing had been mounted on the door frame that she and her brother and sister had used constantly, jumping off once they had made it go as high as it could, with a resulting thump on the floor that would annoy her mother as she sat reading in the room below.

Lila Caner was such an agreeable person, so interested and so complimentary about what we had done to update her childhood home, that I felt sorry I hadn't invited her before. But I also was disappointed that she had nothing to offer with respect to a ghost. In answer to my questions about sounds at night and misplaced objects, Lila said that she occasionally felt nervous when left alone in the house, but no, "I never had any inkling of a ghost."

I decided to return to the Putnam family and to find out what I could about the spinster sister, Anna Cabot Putnam, who had lived in our house for thirty-four years. I returned to the library and found that the microfilm room had moved to a partitioned area at the north end of Bates Hall, where I often worked at the long, lamplit tables. The young woman presiding over the reference materials listened carefully as I stated my business, asking if the obit I sought was for a prominent person. "No," I told her, "but hers was a prominent family, and I think she died around 1920." I requested the appropriate reels for the *Boston Evening Transcript*, the primary repository of death information in those days. Apparently I seemed unfamiliar with library protocol, or just helpless, because she told me to sit down while she filled out a request slip and then fetched the appropriate reel. After I admitted that I hadn't used the new machines, she threaded the film for me and showed me how to focus and make other adjustments. I went to work.

After spinning through many pages of local, national, and international news, as well as ads for Boston retailers, the sports pages, and classified ads, I finally found Anna in the death notices for August 23, 1922. There were only three short and very blurry lines, stating her name, age, and date of death.

Since Anna Putnam had been described as an artist in the house genealogy, I decided to try the Fine Arts Department on the library's third floor. A single floor fan was noisily circulating the damp air (and dust) in the enormous reading room, where paint was peeling off the arched ceiling and falling in large flakes on the dingy carpet. In the alcove containing books of artists' biographies, I pulled out a thick volume titled *Women Artists in America, 1790–1980*, published by Apollo in 1980. Anna Cabot Putnam was not among the artists profiled, and, given the minor status of many who were, I concluded that Anna had not had a professional career, like her friend Madeleine Wynne, but had most likely painted—or sculpted—for her own pleasure. But where? Did she have a studio somewhere in the house? I could not think how to learn anything more about her.

Returning home, I sat in my favorite spot, a chaise in the corner of the dining room, and considered how I might proceed, how I could get a better sense of these people and figure out who had the greater ghost potential. While I had learned some basic facts about former residents, nothing indicated a willingness on the part of any one of them to forsake the peace of the grave for the satisfaction of hanging around our house and moving things. Feeling discouraged and wondering if I were not just wasting time on a ridiculous enterprise, I stared across the hall and into the living room, where the piano that had played all by itself was directly in my line of vision. "Do something!" I muttered. "Show yourself! Give me some hint, a clue to who you might be!" Annoyed and frustrated, for a moment I thought I would just conjure up any lingering ghosts whether they wanted to be conjured up or not.

Eventually I roused my disgruntled self and returned to my office, where I began once more to poke around the ever-expanding archives of Google. It was then that the portal seemed to open, and a whole new group of dead people with strong attachments to our house began to enter via my laptop screen.

First to appear was an architect, not a family member or past resident, but an important figure nonetheless, since this person held the key to the mystery of the original front door. I had punched a random key while scrolling through listings of houses for sale in the neighborhood; I was gathering data for an abatement of our property tax and needed prices of comparable houses. Out popped Lois L. Howe, architect, cited in another new website, backbayhouses.org. Her firm, Lois Howe and Manning, was author of the 1917 renovation.

Going to the website's section on architects, I learned that Lois Lilly Howe, an MIT graduate, had founded Boston's first, and the nation's second, female-led architecture firm. She subsequently added two women draftsmen as partners. Returning to the library, I was able to retrieve Howe's plans and was surprised to learn that many features I had always attributed to the original architect, J. Pickering Putnam, were in fact Howe's work. In particular, the main interior staircase, an elliptical series of flights occupying the center of the house, had been designed by Howe to replace a smaller square flight of stairs. And the original doorway had been placed similarly to most of the others on our street, half a flight up from the sidewalk and to one side; Howe had dispensed with this rote design in favor of a centered garden-level entrance.

In my feminist heart, I was thrilled that a woman was responsible for the alterations that had so transformed our house with added light and space. But I also felt a bit taken aback by what I had just learned. What else had I missed while cruising through the archives of the *Boston Evening Transcript* and other obvious sources? What other assumptions had I made that might be way off the mark? I had spent a good deal more time learning about ghosts and the paranormal than I had on the real people who once lived in our house, and while I felt certain that what I knew about "Uncle Rudy" and his family was accurate, thanks to the notes written out for me by his great-grandniece, I had no direct line to the original owners. I needed to return to Dr. Charles P. Putnam and his family.

I forsook the library and its labyrinthine archives and started with Google. So much had changed in the internet world since I began my fumbling researches years earlier. Now, punching in Dr. Charles P. Putnam, I soon found JSTOR, a digital library of academic journals and publications going back, so far as I could tell, to the invention of the printing press. There was a lengthy remembrance of Dr. Putnam from an unidentified medical journal. The man who subsequently emerged via my laptop screen was fleshed out in a way that made me think this prominent Victorian doctor might be a more benign presence in our raucous contemporary household than I had previously imagined. "So kindly was his disposition, so full was he of sympathy with others whose lot had been harder than his own, so ready to be a worker and, where need was, a fighter for the embodiment of good principles in good institutions, that he found himself . . . plunging more and more deeply into social work." The piece went on in this vein, praising Dr. Putnam for being "a remarkably resourceful man who would reconstruct his patient's world, physically as well as morally, by his calm assumption that anything needed could be done."

Dr. Putnam, who had commenced living in our house with his brother and two sisters, had married Lucy Washburn when he was in his mid-thirties. All I could find about Lucy was her death date, 1926. Charles and Lucy had three children, Charles, Tracy, and Martha; uncertain about whether Tracy (Lucy's mother's surname) was a boy or girl, I Googled Tracy first and learned via Wikipedia that Tracy Jackson Putnam, 1894–1975, was a Harvard-trained neurosurgeon who codiscovered Dilantin, a drug used to control epilepsy. He did critical research on multiple sclerosis at the New York Neurological Institute at Columbia University and was promoted to director. However, "At his time there were quotas for Jewish physicians. He opposed the existence of the quotas. He was forced to resign from Columbia in 1947, maybe because of this. However, other sources mention a 'personal tragedy' Putnam went through at that time (presumably the death of his daughter, Lucy Washburn Putnam, on September 24, 1947)."

Good grief, I thought, *this is a tragic story!* Despite the fact that she had never lived in our house, tragedy is the basis of most paranormal lore, and I couldn't help wonder what happened to daughter Lucy. I went to work and soon learned that Lucy Washburn Putnam had died at age nineteen. A smiling and dimpled dark-haired girl appeared on my screen, alongside a memorial mention in the Vassar College magazine. No cause of death was given, and I could find no other record of Lucy. She would, I figured, have been in the class of 1948 or '49.

Another biographical entry stated that Dr. Tracy Putnam had moved to Beverly Hills, established a private practice, and then become chief of the Department of Neurosurgery at Cedars of Lebanon Hospital in Los Angeles. In a sidebar on the Google page, a wife, Irmarita, was mentioned, as well as a son, Jock, and the movie *The Slime People.* Certain that this was some goofy cross-referencing error, I pursued Jock next, and discovered that he was indeed Tracy's son, and had had a brief acting career, appearing in *The Slime People* in 1963, after which he worked for some years as a boom operator and sound technician. The most recent mention I found for Jock was as "sound mixer" in a 1987 TV movie *Six Against the Rock* with David Carradine.

Tracy's older brother, Charles Washburn Putnam, had been a lawyer, a departure from the usual family career choice of medicine. At first I could find no further information about Charles, other than a notice of his engagement to Miss Dorothy Allen of Commonwealth Avenue, appearing in a 1921 issue of *Town and Country* magazine. Apparently something happened, as Charles married Imogene Phipps Hogle, director of a settlement house in Boston's South End, in 1923 and eventually moved to Ohio. (This was the period of the flu epidemic, and Miss Allen may have succumbed; or it may have been a different Charles Putnam of Back Bay, given the habit of Putnams and their inbred social class to perpetually recycle first names, rather like the kings of England but without the helpful numerals. I found this recycling a real difficulty as I pursued different members of the Putnam family, particularly since they favored "Cabot" as a middle name, as did many of their Brahmin peers. The two most common words in any account of Boston gentry would have to be *Cabot* and *Harvard.*)

I learned more about the older son, Charles, from a new webpage devoted to his daughter, Anne Cabot Putnam, who died in 2012 and who appeared on my screen as a pale blonde with patrician features. Referred to as "Carl," Charles and his wife, Imogene, had Anne the year after his spinster aunt Anna (Cabot) Putnam died, so I assume she was named for the woman who would have been her great-aunt.

C. P.'s third child, Charles's and Tracy's sister Martha, had also followed a medical career, training as a nurse after serving as a nursing aide during World War I. She married Alfred Clarence Redfield, a professor of physiology at Harvard, in 1922, and moved with her husband to Cambridge (it was only through her married name that I was able to trace Martha). They were married for sixty years and had three children, one of whom, Elizabeth, became division chair of natural sciences and mathematics at Stockton State College in New Jersey.

Here was where I should have stopped, having become acquainted with the two generations of Putnams who actually lived in our building: the elder Charles P. Putnam (C. P.), his brother James, and his sisters Elizabeth and Anna; then C. P. and his wife Lucy's children, Carl, Tracy, and Martha. C. P. was the only member of the family to have died in the house, although his sister Anna died several years after having moved a few doors down the street. If my purpose was to gather names of likely suspects for resident ghost, I had exhausted the Putnam possibilities. However, ghost or no ghost, I was captivated by the Putnams and found I couldn't give up poking around their family history just yet. Tracy had stood up to anti-Semitism and produced a son who acted in horror movies. Charles (Carl) had had a daughter who, according to the memorial website, had acted in amateur theater productions and, in the 1970s, adopted a bohemian lifestyle, welcoming people of all colors and classes to party and live in her Manhattan town house. Her sister Mary moved back to Boston and founded the Puppet Showplace in Brookline, where my daughters used to attend performances. What else might I learn about this eminent Boston family?

I suddenly recalled that Dr. James Jackson Putnam, a neurologist, who had lived in our house for ten years, had popped up before in my researches as the first and most noted champion of Sigmund Freud in America. I had been looking for his brother, C. P., but got James as well because he was prominent for, among other things, having founded what is now the Boston Psychoanalytic Institute. Dr. James Putnam, at age sixty-three, heard Dr. Sigmund Freud speak at Clark University, Freud's only American appearance. It had been a life-changing experience for James, and he traveled to Europe to spend time with Freud and his colleagues, subsequently beginning a long correspondence that would be published in *James Jackson Putnam and Psychoanalysis: Letters between Putnam and Sigmund Freud.*

When I discovered a recently published book titled *Putnam Camp*, I promptly ordered a copy.[1] It was subtitled "Sigmund Freud, James Jackson Putnam, and the Purpose of American Psychology," and I hoped to glean some additional facts about those members of the family who had lived in our house. The author, George Prochnik, was identified as the grandson of Dr. James Putnam's daughter Elizabeth; her daughter (Prochnik's mother) had married a Boston man whose father, a doctor, was an Austrian Jew from Vienna. Mr. Prochnik would be the great-grandnephew of C. P. Putnam. But Prochnik's book, as its title implies, is really about psychology and his great-grandfather's relationship with Sigmund Freud, who, during his one US visit, spent three weeks at Putnam Camp, the family's rustic vacation retreat in the Adirondacks.

Hoping I would learn something about Anna, the spinster sister, I read all 455 pages, including acknowledgments and chapter notes. Unhappily, Anna is not mentioned by name, only obliquely in a quote from a letter psychologist William James, a colleague and close friend of James Putnam, wrote to his novelist brother, Henry, in which C. P.'s children are referred to as "an absolutely happy family."[2]

What I did learn from Prochnik was how the family lived and who they were within the context of late nineteenth- and early twentieth-century Boston. A Boston aphorism says that people with family and money lived on Beacon Street, people with family but no money on Marlborough, and those with money but no family on Commonwealth Avenue. The Putnams would have been living proof, being well born but not well off. And while they no doubt belonged to the Harvard and Somerset clubs, there is no evidence that the Marlborough Street Putnams partied or attended cultural events; they seemed to have been occupied with social work more than social life.

Further, this was a time of rapid population growth in Boston, as waves of immigrants arrived and settled in an area of tenements still known as "the North End." Earlier I had read of C. P.'s forays into this morass of tenements, accompanied by his architect nephew, J. P. Putnam, seeking together to improve the health and housing of the city's poor. From Prochnik I learned that the Putnam family was not unique in its dedication to public service; it was part of the zeitgeist for their class and generation. Within this context, however, the Putnams were real activists, working specifically to replace conventional almsgiving with an organization, Boston Associated Charities, that would deliver a range of services centered around moral and practical guidance. Delivery of this guidance was accomplished via personal visits to the poor in their homes.

As I read about the early Putnams and began to visualize the life they led—bustling purposefully about the narrow Boston streets in plain, much-worn clothing, dining on spartan fare, and living in rooms that would have been furnished with a view toward function rather than comfort or beauty (Prochnik includes a bit of a letter in which James Putnam's house is described as bare and rather shabby)—I suddenly remembered Mrs. Gardner, founder of Boston's Gardner Museum and a close Putnam neighbor at 152 Beacon Street. This was also the Gilded Age, and wealthy, socially prominent, New York–born Isabella Stewart Gardner might have lived, not around the corner, but on another planet. Her house, a double-width mansion built as a wedding gift from her father, was stuffed with art and antiques; the windows and walls were draped with brocade. She dressed and entertained extravagantly, even though one of the main rules of Boston Brahminism was to behave discreetly. Numerous members of Boston high society enjoyed Mrs. Gardner's hospitality. Were any of the Putnams ever among them?

I can't imagine that the Gardners and the Putnams didn't cross paths somewhere, both belonging to Boston's insular upper class, and having a significant link in the novelist Henry James. James was one of Mrs. Gardner's circle, a frequent guest at her table and, for a brief time, a neighborhood resident. His novel *The Bostonians*, published in 1885, is set in the milieu of the female Putnams, and his heroines are activists concerned with social reform and the proper role of women in society. Olive Chancellor, the main female character, is portrayed as a woman who eschews marriage and society in favor of hands-on social work. She would have blended quite amicably with the Putnam ladies and no doubt was modeled on women like them.

While I like to think of C. P. and James at one of Mrs. Gardner's soirees, it is hard for me to envision their wives decked out in velvet and serious jewelry, and I suspect that contact among the men occurred within the context of their clubs and professional lives. But there must have been some kernel of interest, some spark of curiosity, among the Putnam women. Isabella Gardner, who is said to have borrowed lion cubs from the zoo so that she could walk them down Beacon Street on a leash, would have seemed like some bizarre mash-up of Brooke Astor and a Kardashian, combining social credentials, wealth, and philanthropic largesse with the behavior of a celebrity show-off. Surely they would have walked around the corner and stared at the Beacon Street mansion, hoping for a glimpse of their flamboyant neighbor.

Reviewing what I had learned about the Putnam family, and thinking about who I would *like* to have as a resident ghost, I found myself drawn back to Tracy. For me, he stood out from the rest. Was it because of his many medical accomplishments? The Croix de Guerre he was awarded by the French for his heroism in rescuing wounded soldiers during World War I? His compassion with respect to Jewish and female colleagues, his many heartbreaks, or just because he had a son who acted in *The Slime People*? Looking once more at the Google listings for Tracy, I found a 2012 piece on the multiple sclerosis webpage, a feature letter from the director titled "Dr. Tracy Putnam and Vascular Research of MS." Despite the unpromising title, the letter proved to be a poignant testament to the contributions, and unjust treatment, of Dr. Tracy Putnam. Written by "Joan," the letter begins by pointing out that the founder and first director of the National MS Society, Dr. Tracy J. Putnam, is never acknowledged or mentioned, despite his having identified blocked veins as a critical factor in the onset of MS, a finding that researchers are just now corroborating. She explains that he was dismissed because his research had produced a theory, not a cure, but also because he refused to fire the "non-Aryan" members of his department: in a recently discovered 1961 letter, Dr. Putnam reported that the head of Columbia's affiliated hospital had told him "that I should get rid of all the Jews in my department or resign."

As I read about Tracy and the rest of the Putnam family's lives and careers—particularly the women, Tracy's wife, Irmarita, and James's daughter, Marian, who managed to enter and finish medical school in those pre–affirmative action days—I kept thinking about a piece in the "Food" issue of the *New Yorker* magazine, in which John Lanchester bemoans the seriousness with which foodies take themselves, how critical they regard their grocery shopping choices to the health of the planet. "Imagine you die and go to Heaven and stand in front of a jury made up of Thomas Jefferson, Eleanor Roosevelt, and Martin Luther King, Jr.," Lanchester writes. "Your task would be to compose yourself, look them in the eye, and say, 'I was all about fresh, local, and seasonal.'"[3] I thought of myself in front of a jury of Putnams, similarly called to account for my contributions to mankind. It would be hard to even look them in the eye.

Despite my being no closer to solving the mystery of the hairbrush or the piano or the pushing on the stairs, my sense of frustration and futility had retreated. Instead I felt grateful that my detour into Putnam genealogy had led me to these remarkable people, and proud to be connected to them, even if it were only through real estate.

❧

CHAPTER FIFTEEN

THE ENFIELD AND OTHER POLTERGEISTS

Periodically I ask myself why I continue to try to solve the mystery of the hairbrush. It has been a long time, years, since any incidents have occurred or I have felt a presence in the house. I think of all the reading I've done, all the people I've talked to, and while my knowledge of the paranormal is now considerable, what do I really know? More to the point, what can I say I believe?

I began my research—or should I say investigation?—with a question: Are there ghosts? This was the big, overriding question, because if I concluded that ghosts did not exist, I would have to go elsewhere for explanations for the mysterious movement of hairbrushes and beds in our house. Early on I submitted an account of these strange goings-on to my writing group at Radcliffe Seminars. Our seminar leader, a poet and longtime teacher, was both a diligent critic and enthusiastic supporter of our writing efforts. After the critique, I began answering questions, and it was then that Alan, suddenly realizing that I was not writing fiction, interrupted. "Am I hearing correctly," he asked, eyebrows raised, "that you believe in ghosts?"

I replied that I believed in the *possibility* of ghosts. As of this moment I can say that I believe in ghosts, not just the possibility. But this is not a simple and unqualified admission. Belief in ghosts implies a belief in some sort of existence after death, and there are variations of afterlife to consider. I must ponder what form this existence might take: An amorphous oneness of our disembodied souls with the universe? A return to the original Garden of Paradise, some kind of eternal lawn party? Or, as I was taught as a young Catholic girl, post-Judgment dismissal to hell, or admittance to the far more exclusive realm of heaven?

And there are versions of ghosts—spirits, poltergeists, apparitions—and associated behaviors, such as telekinesis (moving objects with the mind) and demonic possession, as well as the entourage of paranormal specialists who bridge the considerable gap between the living and the presumed dead: psychics, mediums, clairvoyants, spiritualists. While I am inclined to credulity where many of these entities and practices are concerned, I also know that there is a lot of dubious material perpetrated by amateur ghost hunters, fortune-tellers, and outright frauds. But I am convinced that at least some people are able to communicate and act—or to generate communication and action—after physical death. How this works I cannot say, but I know it does, based on a single experience.

One September morning the sound of "Cuckoo! Cuckoo! Cuckoo!" awakened both my husband and me an hour before dawn. We both heard it and we both knew the sound came from no local or living bird, but from a small wooden one who lived nine hundred miles away, inside Don's mother's clock. Millie's clock, with its silly bird popping out every hour, was a long-standing family joke. Millie had been dead for several years, but she had found a way to let us know that Bill, whose death was expected, had died. Five minutes later, the phone rang.

While my belief in ghosts has evolved from an accumulation of research and personal experience, this one incident suffices: I heard the cuckoo, Don heard the cuckoo; there are no cuckoos in north central Massachusetts.

Nonetheless, I have to bolster my own position from time to time with a reminder that there is other well-documented evidence of ghostly phenomena, and for this reason I was glad to be reminded of the Enfield Poltergeist, revisited in a recent issue of the *Ghost Club Journal.*

The Enfield Poltergeist refers to a series of incidents that occurred in the north London suburb of Enfield during 1977–78. A family living in a modest row house was not just haunted but terrorized by a demonic poltergeist (the variety of ghost that, while generally invisible, makes itself known by making noise and moving things). A friend had introduced me to this case several years ago, and I watched clips of video taken during the investigation on my laptop; recently I read a book-length account of the case written by one of the investigators, Guy Lyon Playfair, *This House Is Haunted.*[1] A series of intense and very dramatic events was observed, photographed, and tape recorded throughout the period of haunting; this formal record of the paranormal activity was confirmed by the eyewitness accounts of at least thirty people. The summary I am about to provide is cursory, as I described the Enfield case in Chapter 5; it may be confusing, but that is because so much happened, so many different people were involved, and so much documentation exists: the investigators' daily journals; photographs, videos, and tape recordings; Mr. Playfair's very detailed book; newspaper accounts; and various articles and interviews in the *Ghost Club Journal.*

The Enfield case began in August 1977, in a semi-detached house in a working-class London neighborhood, home to a divorced mother, Mrs. Harper (a pseudonym), and her four children. The two daughters, Janet, eleven, and Rose, thirteen, slept in the same bedroom. The girls were awakened one night by the sound of feet shuffling along the bedroom floor; they called for their mother who, when she entered the room, also heard the shuffling, followed by loud knocks on the wall. Then, while the family looked on, a large chest of drawers began to move away from the wall.

Mrs. Harper called a neighbor and then the police, who were present when activity moved beyond the bedroom, and a kitchen chair began to slide across the floor, an event observed by a stunned Constable Carolyn Heeps.

The next day, Lego pieces and marbles began flying about. Neighbors contacted the *Daily Mirror* newspaper, and a reporter and a photographer were sent to the house. "It did not take very long for them to decide there was something very strange occurring, particularly when [photographer] Graham was struck by a piece of Lego whilst he was taking photographs. The object had left a very visible bruise on his forehead."[2] The light piece of plastic had to have been thrown with extraordinary force.

During the next fourteen months, events would progress from the movement of objects to the sound of a gruff male voice shouting insults and obscenities. Janet and Rose were repeatedly pushed out of bed by unseen hands (although neither was ever hurt by this or subsequent assaults). Every night featured some version of mayhem, making it impossible for the girls to sleep for very long. (An older son was away at a special needs school, and the younger boy somehow slept through.)

While the family moved briefly to a neighbor's house, Mrs. Harper was too poor and too attached to her house and neighborhood to leave; her brother and his family lived several doors away, and the next-door neighbors, who shared a party wall, were considered family. In September Mrs. Harper was put in touch with Maurice Grosse, a retired inventor of electrical and mechanical devices who had recently become an active member of the Society for Psychical Research, the same investigative organization that had been founded in tandem with the Ghost Club a century earlier. Grosse in turn contacted Guy Lyon Playfair, a Cambridge-educated journalist who had done research on poltergeists while living in Brazil. Joined by a photographer, the two men eventually spent over a year virtually living at the Harper house, monitoring and documenting poltergeist activity, which over the months became increasingly bizarre and malicious. Eventually the investigators became targets: while Grosse was attempting to communicate with the ghost by rapping on the wall, a box of cushions shot off the floor and over the bed, hitting him squarely in the forehead.

As the poltergeist phenomena escalated, the researchers noted that it increasingly centered around the younger daughter, Janet. On Janet's twelfth birthday, November 10, 1977, the house became a maelstrom: knives, an ashtray, and a Guinness bottle flew about; a large armchair with Janet in it tipped over. Most spectacularly, a full-size sofa rose up, flipped over, and returned to the floor upside down. Playfair described how this violence continued over the next several days:

"Furniture started turning over the minute she got home from school . . . the sofa going over twice, once while she was sitting on it. To overturn the sofa normally took two people and quite a lot of effort. . . . Early on 12 November, Janet was tipped out of bed together with her mattress, which landed on the floor with her underneath."[3]

By December Janet had become not only the center but

the source of activity. She began having seizures and going into trances, during which she assumed other personas. Later the names she referenced were identified as belonging to former tenants whom she had never known. She would describe, in what seemed like his voice, how one former resident, a blind old man named Bill, had died while sitting in the living room. Then the raspy voice of a man began to come from Janet, speaking loudly and at random, often using foul language.

I felt I needed to take another look at Janet, whom I remembered vaguely from a YouTube video as a slender, brown-haired adolescent. Hunched over my laptop, I went back over scenes featuring the distraught mother and daughter Janet, an awkward-looking girl with lanky brown hair, bangs, slightly protruding teeth, and what seemed to me to be an increasingly loony expression. I wondered why these people didn't simply leave. How could they sleep? How could the girls do homework? Wasn't Mrs. Harper spending all day putting flying Legos and somersaulting chairs back where they belonged? But the fact was that the Harpers lived in government housing, largely on subsidies, and so had no other options, even if they hadn't been so tied to the neighborhood. A place was found for Janet in a convent residence, and she spent several weeks there, but the mayhem continued as soon as she returned.

Then events proceeded to what was truly a new level: Janet levitated several feet above her bed; a book was thrown at the party wall and subsequently found in a bedroom in the house on the other side, seemingly having passed through the wall; a large red seat cushion was propelled toward a closed window, at which point it disappeared and was observed by a tradesman walking by to reappear on top of the Harpers' roof. The most intriguing account of that day is given by a school crossing supervisor, Hazel Short, who was posted directly across the street from the

Harper house. The house had a large window bay on both the first and second stories, allowing anyone passing by outside to see inside quite clearly when the curtains were open.

"I was standing there looking at the house when all of a sudden, a couple of books came flying across and hit the window (from inside). It was so sudden. I heard the noise because it was so quiet, there was no traffic, and it made me jump.

"When I looked up, a candy-striped pillow hit the window as well. . . . The windows were still closed. Then after a little while I saw Janet. I don't know if there's a bed underneath that window, but she was going up and down as though someone was just tossing her up and down bodily, in a horizontal position, like as if someone had got hold of her legs and back and was throwing her up and down."[4]

After this incident, Grosse and Playfair tested the bed "to see how bouncy it was." They bounced on it but couldn't get in the air, after figuring that Janet had to be at least twenty-eight inches off the bed to be above the windowsill and thus visible from outside.

I include this very brief and incomplete summary of a famous poltergeist case (most recently fictionalized in the 2016 movie, *The Conjuring 2*) because it reinforces what I have come to believe, that there can be ghosts who move things in houses. The Enfield events, over fifteen hundred of them, were not only recorded and often photographed, they were observed by a range of people: not just the family and investigators, but neighbors, journalists, and police officers. And six years later, there was a follow-up investigation by the Society for Psychical Research, whose members interviewed most of the original thirty eyewitnesses.

Frankly, four or five of these incidents, observed and recorded by others, would be sufficient to prove the existence of something otherworldly. These things—the flying Legos, the tipped-over sofa, the voices, Janet's levitation—happened, and they are as well documented as any historic event. I am convinced. Nonetheless, public and professional response to the Enfield case demonstrates why little serious thought or support has been given to those who traffic in the paranormal. Early on various journalists and psychologists, when called to the scene, charged the Harpers, and specifically Janet, with fraud: the girls were "playing games," Janet was "a skilled ventriloquist," and so on. (The investigators worked long and hard to disprove the latter charge, even taping over Janet's mouth, during which time a deep loud voice continued to emanate from her throat.) And no one claimed to understand how the family managed to raise heavy furniture off the ground and flip it.

In March of 1978, Grosse and Playfair presented the Enfield case to a major SPR conference at Cambridge University. After a series of papers on laboratory experiments, which Playfair later described as "duller than any lectures I sat through as an undergraduate," he described Grosse's presentation to over one hundred of their assembled colleagues.

He kicked off with a very concise and factual account of the case to date, summarizing the types of phenomena they had observed or recorded from eyewitnesses. These included knocks, movement of small and large objects, interference with bedclothes, appearance of water, apparitions, levitation of persons, physical assaults of several types, automatisms, psychological disturbance, equipment malfunction and failure, the passage of matter through matter, unidentifiable voice phenomena—both embodied and disembodied—and spontaneous combustion (two matchbooks burned on the outside without the matches themselves igniting).

After playing a selection of recordings from the Harper house, and making a plea for further research into such phenomena by paid professionals, Grosse and Playfair invited questions. They were dismayed when one question after another focused on particular incidents: how many of these had been observed by outside witnesses, and how specific events might have been staged by the Harpers. "All they were interested in was fraud and statistics," Playfair later commented.[5]

Why would those who profess an interest in ghostly phenomena recoil when faced with evidence of same?

I recalled Dr. Daryl Bem, the social psychologist from Cornell, who was ridiculed and ostracized by his colleagues for research that seemed to offer definitive proof of extrasensory perception, a significant percentage of his subjects being able to guess the content of hidden images. After reading about Dr. Bem, I discovered instructional tapes on YouTube that demonstrate how one may learn to move objects telepathically; the segments I watched showed people moving pencils and folded paper, beginner stuff, but the implication was that humans have this ability, or at least some do. (I tried to move a pencil, staring at it determinedly for several minutes, but I could not get it to budge. I blame my failure on a lack of the right kind of concentration and on my oversight in not preparing by clearing my mind beforehand.)

The Enfield Poltergeist raises a number of questions, but the ones that interest me are those related to my own comparatively pallid case. Aside from reinforcing my belief that ghosts exist and we most likely have one, what does this demonstration of actual poltergeist activity really mean? How does it work?

I'd liked to think that our ghost is one with poltergeist tendencies, given the movement of objects, and that it is rather benign, as most poltergeists are. I have also allowed myself to assume that it is the spirit of a former resident. But what if it isn't? The psychic Lorraine told me that we had a portal in the house through which spirits were entering, not necessarily ones with any connection to our house. And Janet, during the course of the Enfield Haunting, was possessed by at least three different entities, only one of whom claimed to be a former resident of the property.

Enfield raises the troubling issue of poltergeists and adolescent girls. No one I've encountered in my reading claims to understand why these ghosts are drawn to pubescent females, other than that they may have a particularly high level of energy and are in a stage of physical transition. Even Playfair suggests that, in some instances, the girls themselves are consciously attracting this activity, even that they have the power to instigate movement of objects. Again, it is not clear to me how this works. But I have to consider the fact that much of the activity in our house occurred when Laura and Elizabeth were young girls living at home. Were they complicit in any of the mysterious events, however unwittingly?

Playfair writes regarding poltergeists: "Is it really a spirit? Is it really something discarnate to the living or is it some mysterious phenomena actually generated by the subconscious mind of living people?" Further, "poltergeists can be interpreted in so many ways and they are not all compatible and the plain fact is we don't really know what they are."[6] While under the spell of whatever possessed her, Janet Harper said things that she could not possibly have known. And it was proven by investigators that she could not possibly have lifted herself two feet in the air, as she was observed to be doing by the passing school crossing guide.

It appears, then, that if I say I believe we have a ghost with poltergeist tendencies, I don't really know what I am claiming, because *poltergeist* is a term without a specific definition—it can be a ghost; it can be an event, like an earthquake, but with as yet unknown causes; or it can be something else, a telekinetic effect produced by the subconscious. According to Playfair, who was interviewed at a Ghost Club meeting in 2015, "poltergeist" is more about things happening than about what makes them happen. As I thought about what went on with young Janet, who spoke in strange voices and said strange, often profane things, what ailed her seemed like some variation of demonic possession, as she was both the agent and the victim of an inexplicable force. Playfair states in the interview that Janet's saying things she couldn't have known, such as the cause of death of a previous resident, implies the involvement of an external entity, but she also seemed to function as a medium, channeling voices of random dead people. Playfair referred to the movie *Ghost*, where Whoopi Goldberg transitions from fake medium to genuine medium: "All these spirits started queuing up to speak through her like waiting to use a public telephone."[7]

Like much of scientific inquiry, one answer generates a lot more questions.

Eventually Janet was freed from the Enfield Poltergeist by a medium recruited from Holland. He took Janet out for ice cream and during that time apparently dealt with whatever issues she was having. He returned to the house and spent some time alone upstairs. "It's gone," he said on his way out the door. The poltergeist, or its effects, subsequently vanished. The medium said little afterward, except that he had had to go to the "astral plane," a place I have come to think of as being a kind of halfway house between earth and heaven, a dimension populated by spirits who have not yet moved on. Apparently some mediums can take themselves there in order to do business with a particular spirit, or to coax a troubled one "into the light," as Echo Bodine might say.

The updatings of the Enfield case, and in particular the SPR follow-up with original witnesses, provided all the necessary proof that I, and I assume most people, require to accept the account as given, not as some elaborate fraud. Those who did not, in the face of such copious evidence, were, in my opinion, merely deniers, that annoying category of skeptics who resist evidence of everything from the Holocaust to climate change. As Playfair points out with obvious irritation, "I think it is time that this sort of evidence is faced up to. Poltergeists challenge everything we think we know about physics, psychology, time, and space, and the evidence has been piling up for at least a thousand years, yet it is still being giggled at by these stupid skeptics who turn up every day on the box and say it can't have happened."[8]

※

CHAPTER SIXTEEN

BACK TO GRAY

I was pulled into the gray, obfuscating atmosphere of skeptics almost as soon as I finished reading the *Ghost Club Journal*'s revisiting of the Enfield case. It was February, and I had flown back from Florida to check on major construction at our house, while staying with good friends who live just around the corner. I had been sitting at the desk in the guest room after dinner, trying to balance my checkbook, when my friend Jody, who knew about my interest in ghosts, walked in and held out her iPad. "Here, I've just finished this movie called *An Honest Liar*," she said, "and I think you should watch it. It's fascinating."

I'd forgotten about James Randi, the magician whose mania for years has been the debunking of psychics and their trade. Much like Houdini, Randi is a conjurer and escape artist of extraordinary talent and fame who abhors the use of the magician's skills for fraudulent purposes. In 2003 Randi had founded an annual conference for scientific investigators, or skeptics, the centerpiece of which is the Million Dollar Challenge, a contest for those who fancy they possess supernatural skills: anyone who could provide evidence of any variety of paranormal ability was eligible to win. No one ever had. Whatever power contestants claimed evaporated on stage.

Born Randall James Zwinge, Randi achieved early fame as an escape artist. His crusade to stop fraudulent use of conjuring tricks went less well until he began offering a prize to those who could prove their claims: $1,000 initially, now $1,000,000 due to considerable outside funding. In 1986 he received a $272,000 MacArthur Foundation Fellowship for his investigative work, prompted no doubt by his successful debunking of Uri Geller, a handsome and charismatic Israeli who had, thanks to performances on shows like *The Tonight Show Starring Johnny Carson*, become famous in the US as a conjurer and mind reader. In 2007 he gave a TED talk on "Homeopathy, Quackery, and Fraud." I had to admit that Randi was a force to be reckoned with.

I settled back into the pillows and propped the iPad on my knees, happy to substitute the movie for the informative but interminable *New Yorker* article I'd planned on reading. Randi appeared on the screen, the former escape artist now a small, wizened man with a long white beard, and began by citing Houdini as his inspiration, both as an escape artist and as a crusader for people's right "not to be duped." Nonetheless, after an hour of the movie I found myself unimpressed with Randi. He showed clips of stage magic, beginning with the old classic where a prone female is levitated some feet above whatever table or platform is supporting her. "Tricks, all basic tricks," he'd say, but he never described or demonstrated the tricks themselves. In the TED talk, he critiqued the practices of psychics via the most dumbed-down examples, describing how their conversations with departed loved ones largely consisted of bromides, such as "I am with all of my dear dead friends and family members," "I am always with you," or "I suffered but now I am happy, together again with my beloved husband." These communications from the dead, according to Randi, are generic and provide no specific or useful information. Well, yes, I thought, but what about my friend Pat and the very specific feedback she received from the psychic Kevin? Kevin, who didn't know Pat until she walked into his office, nonetheless knew everything about her, including how she had just rearranged some seashells kept as a memento of a dead friend. Randi seemed to me to be manipulating the data.

In his TED talk, Randi referred to the work of psychics as "a cruel farce," citing the many victims who had been ruined emotionally and financially. Belief in the paranormal, the occult, and/or spiritualism was "total nonsense, medieval thinking." Here Randi really lost me. Yes, many people have been literally robbed by false psychics peddling false information. (The most recent high-profile case involved a New York man who, heartbroken and desperate when his fiancée left him, spent his life savings, over $700,000, on a psychic who told him whatever she figured he wanted to hear.) But Randi did not acknowledge any legitimate psychics; for him it was all nonsense.

Like so many on both sides of the paranormal debate, Randi seemed to me to have an axe to grind, and while I credit his efforts to protect both his profession and the potential victims of con artists, I sensed that show business was a force in both areas.

Then, just as I finished with Randi and returned to our winter retreat in Miami, I learned of *The Witch of Lime Street*, a recently published account of a famous medium and her career-long battle with Henry Houdini. The book was getting a lot of hometown press coverage because of its Boston setting. I ordered a copy and was soon immersed in the improbable saga of a Beacon Hill matron who became "Margery," a medium as well-known to the newspaper-reading public in the 1920s as Lady Gaga is today.[1]

The "Witch of Lime Street" was Mina Crandon, a.k.a. "Margery," who distinguished herself as a physical medium, one who could not only communicate with the dead but achieve poltergeist-like manifestations—cause furniture and other items to move about—through her spirit contact. Her story was bizarre, as was much else about the 426-page book. Meticulously researched, it was the first publication for its author, David Jaher, a young man trained in theater production and directing who is a practicing astrologer. The cover was a dramatic matte black with lime green trim and white lettering. I discovered quite by accident, after I placed the book on the floor by the bed and turned out my lamp one night, that the letters on the cover, which spelled out *The Witch of Lime Street: Séance, Seduction, and Houdini in the Spirit World*, glowed in the dark. But most intriguing for me was that this was the Lime Street of Beacon Hill. "Margery" had lived and conducted hundreds of séances five blocks from my house.

Born in 1888 in Ontario, Mina Crandon was the wife of a well-to-do doctor twenty years her senior whom she had married after divorcing her first husband, a grocer. She was beautiful, intelligent, and vivacious, interested mainly in dancing and entertaining. Her husband, Roy, was a highly regarded surgeon in obstetrics and gynecology who had developed a keen interest in psychical research; this was not unusual, as many learned men, most prominently William James, had an intense interest in spiritualism, and an accompanying scientist's desire to discover its boundaries. Houdini, the magician and escape artist, was perhaps the most famous performer in the world and certainly the most famous of the medium-busters, pronouncing their profession "nothing more than spook tricks." His close friend Arthur Conan Doyle, just as famous for his authorship of the Sherlock Holmes stories, figures prominently in the book both as an ardent proselytizer for the Spiritualist religion and a devoted supporter of Margery.

In the 1920s, spiritualism was a major pastime as the public flocked to demonstrations of the medium's skill, while popular magazines like *Scientific American* institutionalized skepticism by promoting scientific research as the key to the authenticity of what went on during séances. Official contests of skill were promoted, the forerunners to Randi's Million Dollar Challenge. Men of science literally tested these women (and they seemed mostly to be women), using the crudest of methods—most often some kind of physical restraint (a locked cabinet, limbs bound to their sides)—to discern whether or not the effects realized (disembodied voices, raised tables, floating objects) were achieved via the medium's innate mental powers or by something more mundane, like a hidden gramophone or piano wires.

As I read about Mina, I realized that her career greatly resembled that of the Fox sisters, who had shown early evidence of psychic talent, were promoted and manipulated by others, scientifically tested by experts, and finally forced to discredit themselves. Alcoholism and penury followed. Mina Crandon, after achieving international fame, was similarly brought down, in her case by Houdini, newspapermen, and scientific investigators.

Jaher's book proved much like Playfair's in that he tells the whole story, long and very thorough in its documentation of each and every character, encounter, and séance, every success and setback. I became engrossed in the Mina/Margery story because it includes feats of mediumship that cannot be denied, and is a useful contrast to Enfield in that, while Janet Harper was the recipient of poltergeist attention, Margery was a perpetrator, initiating various otherworldly events after going into a trance. I cannot tell all of Margery's long story here and so will give a broad-brush account of her career. (Readers interested in a detailed account should consult David Jaher's book, an engrossing read.)

As a young wife living on Beacon Hill, with a husband at Harvard Medical School and neighbors busy with their Boston Brahmin social lives, Mina may have been bored. On a whim she went with a friend to see a Spiritualist minister. He was able to summon her brother Walter, whom she had loved dearly and who had died in a tragic accident. After putting her in touch with Walter, the minister told Mina that she herself had strong psychic powers. Mina's husband, Dr. Leroi Goddard Crandon, eager to conduct an experiment around psychic effects, invited four close friends for dinner and a trial séance at their Lime Street home.

Six people subsequently held hands around a wooden table in a small room lit only by a red lantern. These included a physician and his wife, the manager of Dr. Crandon's office building, and a young man traumatized during the Great War who was at the time almost a ward of the Crandons, ostensibly serving as their librarian. As the Crandons and their guests waited in silence, holding hands, tension built. Finally the table began to shake, slide, then rise on two legs. Movement stopped only when Mina left the room. A subsequent séance with four physicians and their wives ended when the table rose. Jaher writes, "According to the séance record, the table pushed [a male guest] out of the den, and through the dark corridor, having smashed into walls and rumpled all the rugs in transit."[2]

In later séances, Mina would go into a trance, and the voice of her brother Walter would be heard, followed by various sounds (music, a bell ringing) and the levitation of objects. This became the pattern: Mina went into a trance, Walter began to speak (and he proved a chatty, entertaining spirit, cracking jokes and poking fun, often whistling or singing), and curious things would begin to happen.

Mina, who never charged for her invitation-only séances, and who took the stage name Margery to protect her privacy, conducted scores of sittings in her Beacon Hill home, many for investigators. By the end of her career, Margery was presiding over séances that had become a showcase for the most extreme in spirit manifestations. Her brother Walter was the presiding spirit, and he prompted musical instruments to play and float about, sitters' hair to be pulled, a bell well out of Margery's reach to be rung, and a wooden cabinet, in which Margery was constrained during a séance, to break apart and crash around her.

These awe-inspiring effects culminated in the appearance of ectoplasm, a substance alleged to emit from spirit mediums via body orifices and form a visible element related to the spirit being summoned. Ectoplasm often appears in old photographs of alleged mediums, a shapeless mass oozing from an ear or nostril, intended as visible proof of the medium's skill; here I would agree with Houdini that it is just "spook tricks." At this point things began to seem sketchy, even to Margery's most ardent supporters, particularly after her ectoplasm took the form of small infant hands during communication with a dead child.

Margery had been investigated almost nonstop during her early years and rise to fame. *Scientific American* had sent a team that included Harry Houdini, and later a group of Harvard doctors and psychologists continued to test her. Arthur Conan Doyle visited Margery and became an enthusiastic supporter; Houdini visited and, while charmed by Margery, insisted she was a fraud and seductress (although later Houdini admitted he couldn't figure out how she achieved some of her more dramatic effects). During the 1920s, she was front-page news in Boston and New York.

What struck me was the nature of the tests given Mina. During séances she was physically constrained, on occasion by ropes but most often by having her arms and legs held by the male sitters. (How did they manage to hold Margery and at the same time hold hands? I wondered.) She was stripped to her knickers and physically searched prior to séances (by female assistants). There were instances when an investigator grasped her thighs to make sure she hadn't concealed some device between them.

Beloved by her spiritualist public, Margery wore herself out performing. By the 1930s she was exhausted, her marriage was failing, and public interest in the occult was waning. Her husband died in 1939 after a fall; Margery, after years of heavy drinking, died alone in the Lime Street house in 1941.

When I returned to Boston from Florida, the first thing I wanted to do was see the Lime Street house. Even if Margery was long gone, the 1890 building itself was almost a character in her saga, for as Jaher says in his account, "It possessed an architectural complexity which surpasses belief. . . . There are two flights of back stairs, affording four independent points of access to the front of the house, there is a butler's pantry with dumbwaiter. The whole house fairly teems with curious closets, crannies, cubbyholes large and small, blind shaftways, etc."[3] Who knows? I might sense a remnant of her spirit, or Walter's, wafting about the area. I set out one afternoon with a list of errands to do—a drop at the shoe repair, light bulbs to pick up at the hardware store, a visit to the ATM in the Santander branch at the corner of Beacon and Charles—and, as is always the case on a mild afternoon, encountered a clutch of picture-snapping tourists outside Cheers, the bar featured in a television series that now attracts many more visitors than Paul Revere's house ever will. The bar is on the ground floor of a stately Georgian building, located at the base of Beacon Hill and across from the

Public Garden. It was late afternoon, and the tourists were joined by a half-dozen young mothers waiting for their children to be dropped by the school bus.

I turned left off Beacon Street and walked the short distance to Lime, a block-long street that is almost hidden, being totally residential and easily missed by those seeking antique shops or restaurants. I couldn't find number 10. The block where the Crandon house should have been went from number 8 to number 12. I could see no evidence that the buildings had been altered or combined. Number 12 seemed too small and number 8 about right, having five stories and, despite an unadorned brick façade, an intimation of spacious rooms within. I thought to go around and see if there were numbers on the back doors, but in this part of Beacon Hill there was no alley, only a passageway closed off by a high gate. I tried the other end of the block but there the buildings joined. There was no access to the rear except for those with keys.

I went home and looked up number 10 Lime on the various real estate sites. It was listed as 8–10 Lime Street, and seemed to have remained a single-family home; the current owner had put the house on the market twenty years earlier and then removed it.

Knowing at least that I had the right building, I went back and studied it more carefully. The outside of the house was, architecturally, dull as dishwater, the brickwork flat and the windows plainly framed, without any period trim or ornamentation. It seemed almost shabby on a block where most of the other houses had been altered to provide larger windows and smart doorways with shiny paint and brass fittings. The building I was studying had a door almost hidden from view, as it was inside an alcove, and nothing in the way of window boxes or decorative plantings. A front window was slightly ajar, revealing a rather dingy roll-up shade. From across the street I could see a light burning toward the back of an otherwise dark interior. *Old people live here*, I said to myself, being reminded of the way our house looked when we acquired it from the elderly owners.

Walking home, I realized that there was no plaque on the house identifying it as the former residence of Mina Crandon, a.k.a. Margery. There are plaques all over the neighborhood identifying the residences of famous Bostonians like Isabella Stewart Gardner, Henry Adams, and Julia Ward Howe. Either Mina was forgotten or, more likely, subsequent owners of her house wanted her forgotten, the nature of her career not being congenial to those who preferred to cohabit with the spirits of prominent authors and statesmen.

Mina's former house told me nothing, but as I considered her career and that of the Fox sisters, I began to understand why those who commune with spirits are so often discredited. Whether fraudulent or genuine, mediums often feel a need to embroider their basic telepathic powers, adding on "effects" that are engineered by themselves or collaborators. There is a porous boundary, it seems to me, between mediums and magicians. Spectacular effects become part of the show. Yes, the way you pulled that rabbit out of a hat is amazing, but what else can you do? Margery, pressed by her husband and the incessant probing of investigators, became complicit in spirit manifestations that were contrived—I strongly suspect by her husband—in particular the tiny hands that appeared on the séance table, supposedly materializing from ectoplasm, later suspected to be formed from very real calves' liver. This piece of Margery lore may be spurious, but it tells me that at some point she felt she couldn't count on her own abilities to impress sitters, and so upped the ante.

I tried to picture the distinguished company—Harvard professors, medical school faculty—traveling from their classrooms and operating theaters to a colleague's house on Beacon Hill—proper enough up to this point—where they would enter a dark room, clasp one of their hostess's bare limbs, and wait for her to receive a presence from the great beyond. Hard to imagine, given these were not members of an obscure cult or secret society. I assume they discussed whatever happened the next day over lunch at the Somerset or Harvard Faculty Club.

I had to wonder also how Margery's husband continued to allow such physical and emotional abuse of his wife. In the face of what seem to me to have been a couple of truly lecherous investigators, more interested in exploring Mina's body than Margery's effects, he maintained a position of defiant truth-seeking, a determination to prove that his wife was the real thing. He also maintained his post of chief of surgery. How did he have the time? There was something odd and rather creepy about Dr. Crandon.

I also wondered about the author, David Jaher, who spent years researching and writing the book, and who also has worked as a professional astrologer, one who makes predictions about the future based upon the position of stars and planets. Jaher keeps a scholarly distance, arranging all the facts, but not interpreting them, except within the context of history. What does he think about Mina, and how did he find her? *Was* Margery the real thing? Jaher reveals nothing of himself, his opinion, only what can be expressed in the words and writings of others. In an October 17, 2015, *Boston Globe* interview, he stated that, "I definitely believe in psychic phenomena," but Jaher is noncommittal on the subject of Margery's psychic abilities.

I believe that Margery may very well have been able to channel her dead brother Walter. How else did she summon his voice, as he chatted, joked, sang for her sitters? (But, as a friend pointed out, who else would know whether or not it was Walter speaking?) But reading about Margery helped me understand why psychic phenomena, and their perpetrators, are so often dismissed as false. There is just *too much*. Grosse and Playfair, presenting their colleagues with hundreds of paranormal incidents, generated mostly disbelief, partly because the amount of data was overwhelming. There simply was too great an accumulation to absorb.

If Mina Crandon had stuck to channeling Walter, and let his speaking through her to assembled sitters suffice, the investigators probably would have gone away convinced. But cognitive dissonance set in after so many very odd things began to happen. And if even one event is proven false—those little hands made of liver!—the whole series is compromised, a single fault bringing down even a mountain of ironclad evidence.

I also began to understand, after toting a half-dozen volumes on paranormal subjects around in my book bag, that their authors do the field little good in their choice of packaging. One book I'd read recently, a detailed and thoughtful first-person investigation of a range of paranormal sites and people in England and America, featured a photograph I recognized from the program notes on *The Turn of the Screw*. It's of two figures, a shroud-wrapped skeleton and a heavily whiskered Victorian man, the grinning skeleton enfolding the man in his shroud, the man recoiling, arms raised and eyes rolling. A very silly picture, and what is it doing on the cover of a very serious book? Playfair's book cover has a dark shadowy house and wavy lettering. And there is the glow-in-the-dark Gothic-style lettering on the cover of *The Witch of Lime Street*. I've always objected to these covers because I don't want to be seen reading them; they give a crazy-old-lady impression I'm too vain to allow.

But now I have a different, more substantive objection. All of these writers on paranormal subjects, no matter how rigorous their research and documentation, either choose, or allow to be chosen, cover designs that belong on children's books or horror story anthologies. It's as if the authors don't want to be taken too seriously, to risk being lumped in the category of crackpots, and so allow book jackets that say "What's inside is just more Gothic frippery." As a result, the authors' research and conclusions are trivialized, the legitimacy of documented paranormal phenomena undercut by cheap visuals.

A sofa tipped over, a voice spoke from the grave, a hairbrush moved from a mantel to a desk—these strange happenings are more believable singly, more powerful as discrete events, and more likely to be accepted as truth and pondered for potential causes. Faced with a barrage of phenomena, statistics, examples—whatever—most people seemed inclined to recoil and shut down. And as I consider this, I think perhaps my own case is not so pallid after all, the relatively few events more eloquent for their scarcity.

CHAPTER SEVENTEEN

❧

AMBIVALENCE YIELDS TO ENLIGHTENED BELIEF

So much time has passed since I began my investigative journey that I have begun to doubt my memory. One does not need to be a neurologist to know how, particularly as we age, the accuracy of our recollections can degrade, and I was beginning to have "did this really happen?" moments. I asked Elizabeth once, when she was a teenager, to write down the events she remembered. Luckily I saved her list: "Laura saw Rita in the laundry room on a day when she wasn't supposed to be here. My bed moved out from the wall. In the middle of the night, a hair band I had left on my dresser landed on my bed. Someone folded Keith's laundry when no one was home."

I also have been bothered by my conversation years ago with our live-in sitter Kate, wondering if, when she said there must be "an army" of ghosts, she had in fact been pulling my leg. After a long career in the restaurant business, Kate, now married and the mother of two boys, is the assistant to a well-known novelist. I tracked her down, and we made a date to talk on the phone. "There was a lot of ghost activity," she told me, adding that she had always been sensitive to ghosts. "I would feel things were being moved all the time and it was like someone was playing with you. I would hear things. There was a tension, a feeling I had. It was particularly strong in the third-floor sitting room. I used to go in there and walk around, and I could feel something, a presence, people moving past, and the air got colder." The sitting room Kate referred to was originally the parlor, the house's one communal room, where the Putnam family and their guests read, conversed, and met to discuss how to aid the city's poor.

Needing others' ghost stories to bolster my own, I retrieved my notes of anecdotes shared by friends. My former next-door neighbor Cheryl, who lived in a town house that has been broken into apartments, told me about the apparition of a young woman that would occasionally appear, standing near her bathroom door and looking lost (there would not have been a bathroom in the original high-ceilinged room). My former piano teacher described a man in a Civil War–era uniform she twice found standing in her library, scanning the bookshelves. My favorite is a story my sister-in-law Maggie told me: her younger sister now lives in a house previously owned by an elderly aunt. The old woman used to rest in her rocking chair with a cup of tea each day around four o'clock. She died several years ago, but the chair still rocks, every afternoon.

Enough. I feel it is time for conclusions. My exploration of the paranormal world began with simple curiosity, and then, as I learned more, proceeded through stages of fascination, credulity, skepticism, frustration, recurring ambivalence, and enlightened belief. While I know I can continue my inquiries—there always is more information—I will rest my case at "enlightened belief."

Are there ghosts? Yes, there are. The catch is that I have had to expand and refine my definition of *ghost* to include "poltergeist," a broad, poorly understood branch of spirit activity that seems to manifest itself in disturbances of physical objects, activity that seems, like a virus, to erupt under certain conditions (often featuring unhappy adolescent girls), to run its course, and subside. When I said much earlier that I thought we had a ghost with poltergeist tendencies, I should have underlined "tendencies," because we have never experienced the kind of concentrated and disruptive events that characterize the poltergeist phenomena. And to my definition of *ghost*, I must also include the energy of place, that is, the psychic essence of the former inhabitants of a building which is somehow imbedded in the structure.

Two authors on paranormal subjects I have learned from and been influenced by are Stacy Horn and Will Storr. Stacy Horn began her work on *Unbelievable*, the history of Dr. J. B. Rhine's parapsychological lab at Duke, as a curious, open-minded researcher who had her own ghost story to tell. The vast lab archive contained many accounts of both ESP experiments and extraordinary paranormal events, events that were ignored or declared fraudulent by the scientific establishment. While giving these events her full and evenhanded attention, Horn does not take a personal stand, emphasizing the neglect rather than the veracity of Rhine's findings. Needing something firm to put under her noncommittal conclusions about telepathy and afterlife, Horn quotes Einstein: "The most beautiful thing we can experience is the mysterious."[1] But in an insightful and well-reasoned summing up, Horn declares that there is much more to be learned about consciousness, and that future developments in science will most likely confirm the existence of telepathy, citing "the recent overlap between information theory, quantum mechanics, theories about consciousness, and parapsychology."[2]

Will Storr, author of *Will Storr vs. The Supernatural*, also cites quantum mechanics, but he writes of his newfound belief in ghosts with the passion of a convert. A respected journalist who has embedded himself in various subcultures in order to get a story, Storr embarked on a year-long exploration, during which he experienced firsthand a range of dramatic paranormal events. He began the project with an open, enthusiastic attitude—this was an adventure, something truly bizarre to experience and write about—and ended with a conviction I'm sure he never anticipated: "Because ghosts exist. There really are such things as apparitions and EVP and poltergeists and heavy breathing in old rooms in the night." Further, "You're left with evidence. Genuine, unexplained, skull-buckling fantastic evidence. For me, the extraordinary truth about ghosts doesn't lie in the experiences of one witness or another. It lies in the patterns. That perhaps four or five other people heard the breathing in that bedroom before me . . . makes it one of the most incredible mysteries in the world. . . . I am convinced that one of the frontier sciences will eventually solve ghosts. And most likely it will be quantum theorists."[3]

Events like those that occurred at Enfield and similar events of more limited scope have been happening for years. Most have been witnessed by more than one person and documented. Those observations and documentations should speak for themselves. Somehow they do not, and one of the passions I've developed over the course of my investigation is extreme irritation: How can scientists be so pigheaded? Why will they not look into these things?

Do we have a ghost? Yes, I think we do, because we have experienced events no one can explain. Some have been witnessed by several people; as for other, more personal manifestations, I can only describe the feeling I get, when I sit down in our living room to practice the piano, of someone hovering about at the opposite end of the room. The scientific method is irrelevant; I can only prove the phenomenon to myself by experiencing the same sensation day after day. The rest of you will just have to take my word for it.

We also appear to have the energy-ingrained-in-the-walls type of ghost. Three years after finishing college, Laura was back in her old room, living at home while working at Massachusetts General Hospital, taking night courses, and preparing to apply to medical school. Laura began saying she wanted to be a psychiatrist when she was in the eighth grade; she never wavered from this ambition, and a psychiatrist (specializing in geriatric psychology) is what she is today. We have no medical people in Don's or my family, or medical history that includes psychiatry. Where did this ambition come from? When friends asked about Laura's career choice, I used to joke that it was the neighborhood: so many psychiatrists and psychologists live and practice here and the Boston Psychoanalytic Institute is just around the corner. It must be vibrations!

Now I wonder if there isn't something in this, and if the critical influences aren't even closer to home, given that our house was occupied by men practicing psychiatry for all but ten of the 102 years prior to our arrival. Are the spirits of Dr. Putnam and his psychiatrist brother James, and of Dr. Caner, a psychiatrist who saw patients in the first-floor room I now use as an office, dwelling among us? I believe some part of their particular energy remains inside these walls.

Who is our ghost? I don't know and can only make an educated guess. It could be any of the people I've just mentioned, one of their many family members, or a servant I cannot trace. It is purely speculation, but I have always favored Anna, Charles and James Putnam's spinster sister and one of the original inhabitants of our house. She lived most of her adult life here, from 1875 to 1914, and no doubt had close contact with the Putnam children, sleeping on the same floor as the nursery (now Laura's bedroom). Unhappily, as I reported in an earlier chapter, I know very little about her, other than that she was an artist. I continue to search for information on Anna Putnam.

My long journey through the paranormal world has raised questions other than my original ones, most prominent being those related to science, religion, and afterlife. These are topics I am not prepared or qualified to address, but since these threads are visible throughout the fabric of this book, I can't leave them dangling.

The author Alan Lightman is uniquely qualified to comment on these questions, being a member of both the science and humanities departments at MIT (he teaches theoretical physics and creative writing), who has in *The Accidental Universe* considered the remaining mysteries of the world we live in. Lightman describes those who believe that the mind and consciousness are solely functions of the brain as *mechanists* and those who believe that there is "a special quality of life—some immaterial or spiritual force—that enables a jumble of tissues and chemicals to vibrate with life" as *vitalists*.[4] Lightman, who identifies himself as a mechanist, nonetheless endorses religion and belief in the supernatural as legitimate for those whose personal experience has given rise to religious beliefs. For proof that the higher echelons of science can include such individuals, he quotes Harvard's Owen Gingerich, emeritus professor of astronomy and the history of science: "I believe that our physical universe is somehow wrapped within a broader and deeper spiritual universe, in which miracles can occur."[5] For a deep, thoughtful study of the nature of consciousness, and of the reconciliation of religious and scientific beliefs, I emphatically recommend Lightman's book.

With respect to afterlife, for me the problem is not whether it exists, but what, exactly, it is. Where does our ineffable spirit go? "Afterlife" is a rather abstract notion that for most is synonymous with the slightly more specific notion of heaven. Ghosts and spirits are, while chatting with mediums and others, maddeningly tongue-tied when it comes to describing their day-to-day surroundings. And most of the living have a vision of heaven that hasn't been updated since childhood. What afterlife, or heaven, actually looks like has not been reliably reported, since we've only heard from those recently or nearly dead, who seem to have been in a white tunnel or some kind of waiting area, like the characters in *Our Town*. Dead people speaking through mediums have not focused on their physical surroundings. Possibly there aren't any physical surroundings.

Whatever idea of afterlife we may have, from the point of view of the living, it is mostly about an absence of bad things (pain, loss, fear), with the void being filled by good things (bliss, contact with loved ones). Thornton Wilder, however, cautioned that we would do better to focus on our life as we are living it. Heaven may not be all that it's cracked up to be.

My own belief in ghosts and spirits stems in large part from what I have learned, not just about the paranormal world, but about the world of science, specifically about the conservation of energy. According to Lightman, "although energy can change form, its total amount remains constant." We may not die at all, then, just change our shape. Matter is always present in some form, and our skin and bones may be reduced to sand or ashes or worm casings; to what is the energy of our soul, our spirit, reduced or transformed? *That* is a mystery.

Earlier in this book I referred to Henry James's famous ghost story, *The Turn of the Screw*. This is a tale of the possession of two children by the demonic ghosts of former servants, a tale told by their governess, now dead, to a man, now also deceased, who shared the account with a group of his friends. Writers, critics, and readers have argued over the years about James's intentions, whether the reader is to accept one interpretation or another—that the governess imagined it all or that the ghosts existed—or to consider that both the governess's mental problems and the existence of demonic spirits are equal possibilities. In a *New Yorker* essay, however, the critic Brad Leithauser dismisses the idea that a single interpretation is required. He describes *The Turn of the Screw* as "a modest monument to the bold pursuit of ambiguity."[6]

That is how I have come to think of my efforts to get at the truth of the ghost business, because as convinced as I may sound when I say yes, there are ghosts, and we have at least one living with us, in my heart I know that this conviction is conditional, inevitably subject to new information. While we can't help but think of our twenty-first-century selves as close to knowing it all, we may be somewhere in the middle of a vast learning curve, with Copernicus and Galileo not that far behind. Recently scientists have been presented with a new truth, that we are part of a multiverse, and that there are likely other worlds, other constellations, with different forms of life and different laws of nature. A long-held belief that we on earth are the center of the one and only universe has had to yield to new information.

Someday, confronted with a different, more plausible explanation, I may have to revise my belief that it was a ghost who hid the hairbrush.

We've had no activity in several years, not, it occurs to me, since Laura married and Elizabeth moved to New York. I sometimes wonder if our ghost has left for good. The girls' bedrooms are empty, and Don and I are away much of the time.

Everyone is home for major holidays, though, and we

continue to spend Thanksgiving at our house in the country. This past year everyone managed to arrive Wednesday evening, so we had all of Thanksgiving Day together; Don, Craig, and Laura left early for work on Friday while Liz and I stayed behind with sixteen-month-old Alex. The plan was for everyone to reconvene in Boston that evening and spend the weekend in town.

Friday morning Liz and I managed to straighten the house, pack up leftovers, and feed Alex by noontime; we strapped him into his seat for the ninety-minute drive, hoping he would sleep all the way. He didn't, and knowing he'd be fussy if he missed his nap, when we arrived Liz carried Alex upstairs and put him in his crib. After twenty minutes he began to cry, so Liz went back upstairs and brought him down to the kitchen.

As she strapped Alex into the high chair, I noticed his stock-inged feet, and recalled that he had been wearing the little blue Crocs I'd recently bought him. I started up the two flights of stairs, assuming the shoes had been left in the small bedroom next to Laura's, where we have installed a crib and some of her old books and toys. One blue shoe was on the floor near the crib, but I didn't see the other one. After sifting through the blankets, looking under and around the crib, and searching the canvas tote that held his clothes, I went back downstairs.

"Where did you put the baby's shoes?" I asked Liz. "I only found one."

"I put both shoes together right under the crib."

"Did you let him walk around a bit before you came down?" I knew that Alex sometimes carried his shoes around, and he might have dropped one somewhere.

"No, he was really wailing. I picked him up out of the crib and brought him straight downstairs."

"Well, did you take him in your room first and maybe one of them fell off?"

"No, Mom. I didn't put his shoes back on."

"Are you sure?" I persisted, not wanting to go upstairs again.

"Yes, Mom!" Liz was adamant.

"Humph." I puffed back up the two flights. From the doorway I scanned the small room, then got down on my knees. I crawled around, thinking Liz might have inadvertently kicked one of the shoes under the chest next to the crib. I looked under the crib again, under the daybed that sat along one wall, and under the armchair near the window that held an assortment of stuffed animals. Then I looked behind the chair.

There, just under the windowsill, was the missing shoe. A small blue Croc was wedged between one of the chair's legs and the wall. It was a place where, if he wanted to look out the window, a small child just might have dropped it. But if Liz was telling the truth—and why wouldn't she be?—no child we knew had been there.

ACKNOWLEDGMENTS

My outstanding debt is to my writing group, which began at Radcliffe Seminars many years ago, and continued independently when the program ended. Membership dwindled over the years until only four of our original group remained: Terri Butler, Gwynne Morgan, Henriette Power, and myself. This past year Elizabeth Marcus joined us. All of these writing colleagues have provided critical guidance and support.

I must single out Terri Butler, who died on April 13, 2018. Without fail, Terri read carefully, writing comments that were always insightful, thoughtful, and somehow comforting. That her penetrating remarks were above all *helpful* is demonstrated by how frequently I referred to them as I revised my book.

I must also thank Annette Wenda, the editor I didn't think I would need. She has corrected and sharpened my prose and made me feel far happier with my manuscript than I would have been without her.

Last of all, appreciation goes to my daughters, Laura and Elizabeth, and to my husband, Don. Don has patiently endured my preoccupation with this project. His has been the support of an unqualified fan, for everything I do.

NOTES

CHAPTER THREE

1. Echo L. Bodine, *Relax, It's Only a Ghost* (Gloucester, MA: Fair Winds Press, 2001).
2. Jon Izzard, *Ghosts* (New York: Octopus Books, Hachette Book Group USA, 2010).

CHAPTER FOUR

1. Jon Izzard, *Ghosts* (New York: Octopus Books, Hachette Book Group USA, 2010), 79.
2. Paul Chambers, *Paranormal People: The Famous, the Infamous and the Supernatural* (London: Blandford Press, 1998).

CHAPTER FIVE

1. Adam Curtis, "The Ghosts in the Living Room," *The Medium and the Message* (blog), BBC, December 22, 2011, https://www.bbc.co.uk/blogs/adamcurtis/2011/12/the_ghosts_in_the_living_room.html.

CHAPTER SEVEN

1. Benedict Carey, "Top Journal Plans to Publish a Paper on ESP, and Psychologists Sense Outrage," *New York Times,* January 6, 2011, A1 and A3.
2. Stacy Horn, *Unbelievable: Investigations into Ghosts, Poltergeists, Telepathy, and Other Unseen Phenomena, from the Duke Parapsychology Laboratory* (New York: Ecco, an imprint of HarperCollins, 2010).
3. Horn, 2–4.
4. Horn.

CHAPTER EIGHT

1. Oliver Sacks, *Hallucinations* (New York: Alfred A. Knopf, 2012), x1.
2. Sacks, 224.
3. Sacks, 227.
4. Sacks, 231–2.
5. Sacks, 233.
6. Sacks, 247.
7. Sacks, 160.
8. Sacks, 250.
9. Sacks, 235.
10. Philip Carr, *Ghost Club Journal*, Issues 1–20B, 24–26.
11. Eben Alexander, MD, *Proof of Heaven: A Neurosurgeon's Journey into the Afterlife* (New York: Simon and Schuster Paperbacks, 2012), 40.
12. Michael Shermer, "Why a Near Death Experience Isn't Proof of Heaven," *Scientific American*, April 13, 2013.
13. Martin Samuels, MD, in "Readers Join Doctor's Journey to the Afterworld's Gates," by Leslie Kaufman, *New York Times*, November 26, 2012, C1.
14. Sacks, *Hallucinations*, 155–158.
15. Alexander, *Proof of Heaven*, 150.
16. Gary Greenberg, quoted in the *New York Times*, May 2, 2013, C2.

CHAPTER NINE

1. Rosemary Altea, *The Eagle and the Rose* (New York: Warren Books, 1995), 56.
2. Altea, 65.
3. Altea, 51.
4. Altea, 37.

CHAPTER ELEVEN

1. William S. Baring-Gould, *Annotated Sherlock Holmes* (New York: Clarkson N. Potter, 1967).
2. Joseph McCabe, *Is Spiritualism Based on Fraud?* (London: Watts & Co., 1920).
3. Malcolm Gladwell, "The Physical Genius," *New Yorker*, July 25, 1999.
4. Henry James, *The Turn of the Screw*, novella first published as a serial in *Colliers Weekly* magazine, 1898.

CHAPTER THIRTEEN

1. T. M. Luhrmann, "When Things Happen That You Can't Explain," *New York Times*, March 5, 2015, Opinion.

2. Barbara Ehrenreich, "A Rationalist's Mystical Moment," *New York Times*, April 6, 2014, Sunday Review.

3. Brian Greene, *The Fabric of the Cosmos* (New York: Alfred A. Knopf, 2003).

4. Philip Kitcher, *New York Times*, Book Review.

5. Tom Stoppard, *The Hard Problem*, play reviewed by Ben Brantley, *New York Times*, January 31, 2015, C1 and C4.

6. A. O. Scott, "To Scientists in Pursuit, a Bit of Matter Is No Small Matter," film review, *New York Times*, March 4, 2014.

7. Gary Marcus, "The Trouble with Brain Science," *New York Times*, July 12, 2014, Opinion.

8. George Harrison, "Ghosts in the News," *Ghost Club Journal*, February 5, 2017, 6–7.

9. Edward Frenkel, "The Reality of Quantum Weirdness," *New York Times*, February 22, 2015.

10. Daniel Engber, "Daryl Bem Proved ESP Is Real, Which Means Science Is Broken," *Slate*, May 17, 2017.

11. Dennis Overbye, "Gods and Truths for Other Inhabited Worlds," *New York Times*, December 23, 2014, D6.

12. Carlo Rovelli, *Seven Brief Lessons on Physics* (New York: Riverhead Books, 2016).

CHAPTER FOURTEEN

1. George Prochnik, *Putnam Camp: Sigmund Freud, James Jackson Putnam, and the Purpose of American Psychology* (New York: Other Press, 2006), 53.

2. Prochnik, 53.

3. John Lanchester, "A Foodie Repents," *New Yorker*, October 27, 2014.

CHAPTER FIFTEEN

1. Guy Lyon Playfair, *This House Is Haunted* (London: Souvenir Press Ltd, 2007).

2. Playfair, 32.

3. Playfair, 76.

4. Playfair, 144.

5. Playfair, 215.

6. "The Enfield Haunting: An Audience with Guy Lyon Playfair," *Ghost Club Journal,* Issue 2-2015, 35.

7. "Enfield Haunting," 41.

8. "Enfield Haunting," 31.

CHAPTER SIXTEEN

1. David Jaher, *The Witch of Lime Street: Séance, Seduction, and Houdini in the Spirit World* (New York: Crown Publishers, 2015).
2. Jaher, 123.
3. Jaher, 160.

CHAPTER SEVENTEEN

1. Stacy Horn, *Unbelievable: Investigations into Ghosts, Poltergeists, Telepathy, and Other Unseen Phenomena, from the Duke Parapsychological Laboratory* (New York: Ecco, an imprint of HarperCollins, 2009).
2. Horn, 240.
3. Will Storr, *Will Storr vs. The Supernatural: One Man's Search for the Truth About Ghosts* (London: Ebury Press, an imprint of Random House, 2006), 307.
4. Alan Lightman, *The Accidental Universe* (New York: Vintage Books, 2013), 120.
5. Lightman, 43.
6. Brad Leithauser, "Ever Scarier: On 'The Turn of the Screw,'" *New Yorker*, October 29, 2012.

ABOUT THE AUTHOR

Phot credit: Susannah Bothe

Jeanne Stanton, former faculty member and associate dean of the Simmons Graduate Program in Management, is the author of *Being All Things,* an account of women's attempts to manage successful careers with their parallel lives as wives and mothers. At Harvard Business School she wrote numerous case studies in the areas of Organizational Behavior and Marketing. Stanton lives with her husband and Scottish terrier, Alice, in Boston's historic Back Bay.

SELECTED TITLES FROM SPARKPRESS

SparkPress is an independent boutique publisher delivering high-quality, entertaining, and engaging content that enhances readers' lives, with a special focus on female-driven work. **www.gosparkpress.com**

Wave Woman: The Life and Struggles of a Surfing Pioneer, Vicky Heldrich Durand. $29.95. 978-1-68463-042-4. *Wave Woman* is the untold story of Betty Pembroke Heldreich—a pioneering champion Hawaii surfer in the mid-1950s, a female athlete, an artist, a professional who broke glass ceilings and believed anything exciting was worth trying at least once, an inspiration to women of all ages.

Even if Your Heart Would Listen: Losing My Daughter to Heroin, Elise Schiller. $16.95, 978-1-68463-008-0. In January of 2014, Elise Schiller's daughter, Giana Natali, died of a heroin overdose. *Even if Your Heart Would Listen* is a memoir about Giana's illness and death and its impact on her family—especially her mother—as well as a close examination and critique of the treatment she received from health care practitioners while she was struggling to get well.

Roots and Wings: Ten Lessons of Motherhood that Helped Me Create and Run a Company, Margery Kraus with Phyllis Piano. $16.95, 978-1-68463-024-0. Margery Kraus, a trailblazing corporate and public affairs professional who became a mother at twenty-one, shares ten lessons from motherhood and leadership that enabled her to create, run, and grow a global company. Her inspiring story of crashing through barriers as she took on increasingly challenging opportunities will have women of all ages cheering.

Love You Like the Sky: Surviving the Suicide of a Beloved, Sarah Neustadter. $16.95, 978-1-943006-88-5. Part memoir and part self-help in nature, this compilation of emails—written by a young psychologist to her beloved following his suicide—chronicles the process of surviving and grieving the tragic death of a loved one, and of using grief for deeper psycho-spiritual healing and transformation.

The Natives are Restless: A San Francisco dance master takes hula into the twenty-first century, Constance Hale. $40, 978-1-943006-06-9. Journalist Constance Hale presents the largely untold story of the dance tradition of hula, using the twin keyholes of Kumu Patrick Makuakane (a Hawaii-born, San Francisco-based hula master), and his 350-person arts organization. In the background, she weaves the poignant story of an ancient people and the resilience of their culture.